Early Years Observation and Planning in practice

Best practice for planning and observation in the EYFS.
Includes guidance on cohort progress tracking and analysis

By Jenny Barber and Sharon Paul-Smith

Introduction	2
All about observations	3
Observation methods	13
All about planning	28
The planning cycle	43
All about assessment	47
Monitoring and reviewing your planning, observation and assessment	51
Cohort progress tracker sheets	53
Observation and planning and your Ofsted Inspection	62
Example assessment sheets for twos	64
Further resources	66

Acknowledgements:

Jenny Welham, NCMA, Network Co-ordinator, North Buckinghamshire. Kim Goldhagen, Leader, Cheddington Pre-School, Buckinghamshire. Corinne Finlay, EYP, Town Hill Early Years Centre, Southampton. Mary Jefferson Cobb, Childminder, Buckinghamshire. We'd also like to thank all the wonderful early years practitioners that we meet in the course of our jobs who have helped in all sorts of different ways with the writing of this book.

Published by Practical Pre-School Books, A Division of MA Education Ltd, St Jude's Church, Dulwich Road, Herne Hill, London, SE24 0PB

Tel: 0207 738 5454

www.practicalpreschoolbooks.com

© 2010 MA Education Ltd. Revised edition printed 2012. Updated edition printed 2014.

Front cover and CD-Rom photo by Lucie Carlier, © 2011 MA Education Ltd.

Illustrated by Cathy Hughes.

Early Years Observation and Planning in practice ISBN 978-1-909280-24-3

Introduction

We decided to write this book having identified a need for a point of reference in relation to planning and observation. We felt that what was needed was a clearer and greater understanding of why you need to observe children in the early years and how observations

Observations are the starting point of a key person's relationship with their key children

then link to planning. The Early Years Foundation Stage (EYFS) asks you just to record what is 'absolutely necessary' to show that children are making progress. This is to prevent reams of unnecessary paperwork being completed and that time is spent with the children. What we have outlined in this book gives a clear guide as to how to interpret the 'absolutely necessary' and how to meet this requirement. This includes giving consideration to ongoing observations, the importance of regular summative assessments and displaying clear links between your observations and planning to demonstrate that you are meeting individual needs.

Observation should not be seen as a chore, but an opportunity to explore the wonder of each child. If you can understand clearly the purpose and reasoning behind your observations, then the ability to observe and interpret observations will fall into place.

That understanding of what to look for in an observation will help to develop an awareness of what to watch out for and what that might mean for each child's learning and development. This should aid you in deciding what experiences, activities and resources to plan for a particular child or a group of children.

Observations are the starting point of a key person's relationship with their key children; they help practitioners to get to know and understand the children, and cement the adult-child relationship. Ultimately the relationship practitioners have with their key children helps children to feel secure and happy in the setting and supports their learning and development potential.

Planning can be seen as an onerous task, but if you allow yourself to be flexible and spontaneous and let the children guide you in terms of what you plan, the whole process becomes much simpler.

How to use this book

This book is divided into key sections, each of which deals with one aspect of the process of observation and planning. Each can be seen as separate, but all aspects need to be put in place in order to ensure that each child's learning and development is supported through challenging activities.

The accompanying CD-Rom contains proforma assessment and observation forms to help you in creating your own. Each form is designed as a basic guide rather than a prescriptive outline, and each is designed to be adapted to the needs of your particular setting. Remember, paperwork should only be used if it benefits children: it is not there as 'proof' for your manager or inspectors, but rather as an aid to your own planning and observation, to ensure that the needs of each child are recognised and met.

All about observations

The reasons for observation

Observations have always been considered as an essential part of good childcare practice. It is through observations that you get to know the child and use that knowledge to guide you in the provision of experiences. The Department for Education and Skills publication *Starting With Quality* (1989) states that:

> '*A good educational programme for under fives will offer ample opportunities to observe closely and to assess children's learning.*'

> '*....collaborative planning which is based upon observation based assessment of children in all areas of development.*'

More recently in the DCSF (2009) publication *Learning, Playing and Interacting*, it states that:

> '*[P]ractitioners observe children's activities carefully, trying to discover what the child is thinking about and learning and the goals of the play, so they can accurately support and extend the child's learning focus either at the time, or by later changes to the environment or in planned activities.*'

As an early years practitioner you need to reflect and identify how you observe effectively within the setting, to aspire to be the best and most effective in your systems and processes of observation, as this will bring about better outcomes for children.

In the documents *A Passion to be Outstanding* (Ofsted, September 2009) for childcare groups and childminders, Ofsted noted that outstanding practice in the area of observation, assessment and planning was seen in settings as:

- Responding to the needs and interests of all children.

- Talking with the parents, carers and children during the admission to find out about children's abilities, likes, dislikes, routine and cultural and family background.

- Establishing starting points from which they track children's development.

- Planning to ensure children have a wide range of opportunities to challenge and to enable them to meet their next steps.

- Involving children in planning.

- Keeping plans flexible and respond to children's changing interest and day to day events.

- Staff knowing children well because they regularly talk about the observations they make in all areas.

- Staff discussing and recording what the observations tell them about a child's interests and progress they are making.

- Staff using clear systems to monitor children's progress towards their identified next steps.

For childminders:

- Recognising that children learn best when they are having fun, interested and excited by what they are doing and building on what they already know.

- Being clear about each child's starting points.

- Frequently observing and assessing the children, so they know what they enjoy doing, their learning journey and their progress.

- Using their knowledge of each child to make good decisions about the next steps in their learning.

- Being flexible to changing circumstances and unexpected events.

- Providing a balance of adult and child-led activities to meet children's individual needs and interests covering all seven areas of learning.

Before we even consider how to observe, we need to think about the reasons why we need to observe and how to set the scene for effective observation. If you are clear about the reasons behind why you observe, you will be more effective in your approach. Knowing the purpose and motivation behind observations gives you a clearer insight and this understanding enables you to identify how to use observations, what to look for and how then to use the information collated effectively.

The following list identifies the key principles behind the practice of observing children:

- To enable you to identify where a child is developmentally, their skills and interests, likes and dislikes, which in turn, enables you to meet their individual needs.

- To identify positive changes in a child e.g. achievement of a particular skill, reaching a developmental milestone, a positive change in behaviour.

- To see how a child works and interacts both individually and as part of a group, with adults and with other children.

- To help identify any problems and issues e.g. relating to behaviour or special educational needs, observations can be used to help identify patterns in behaviour and triggers for certain types of behaviour.

- To use as a tool to share information with parents, other professionals and practitioners who work in another setting the child may attend.

- To support transitions for children, whether that be between rooms in a day nursery or when moving to a new setting.

- To inform planning so that experiences reflect children's needs and interests and contribute towards an effective learning environment.

- To help you identify how a child uses their environment and how they engage in free flow play. Free flow play being where a child is able to move freely between experiences within the environment.

- To identify how children respond and react in different situations.

- To help ensure that you are providing broad and balanced experiences for the child, by reflecting on observations of a child, you can see if they are experiencing all seven areas of learning and development.

- To help you ensure the routine is effective and meeting the children's needs, and the children have a sufficient time for sustained play.

- To identify whether a child may have regressed developmentally owing to an event in their lives e.g. moving house, new sibling, and parental separation.

Where to start

So we know that observations provide early years practitioners with a plethora of tools for supporting practice, and the key to this is ensuring that observations are valid and effective. So where to begin? By getting to know the 'unique child', and establishing starting points. A starting point is where a child is at when they first begin in the setting in terms of their development and skills or if a child is new to you it is where they are now. These starting points are established by the child's parents, information from a previous setting or another setting the child attends, as well as the initial observation you will have carried out. This is recorded on an 'All about me' form, which begins the learning journey (see proforma on the accompanying CD-Rom). The completion of this form can help establish key relationships with the parents, so it is important to complete

Completing the 'All About Me' form together

the form with the parents. The child may not be involved but it will be an opportunity for the child to see the child's parents engaging with the practitioner.

It is important to remember that the child may behave differently during that initial settling in period. After the child has initially settled, usually between 3 and 6 weeks, you will need to think about the following when establishing the starting points:

- What play choices does the child make?

- What can parents tell you about the child's needs?

- What does the child tell you about their own needs?

- How do you know if the child is happy?

- What can the child do now?

- What is the child trying to do next?

- How does the child like to learn?

The basis for this needs to include feedback from parents, perhaps on a settling-in-form (included on the CD-Rom), as well as your own formal and informal observations.

Once you feel you are getting to know the child and are beginning to feel confident about the knowledge you are building about the child, you can begin the process of observations.

What to consider when observing

From a practical point of view you need to consider the following when carrying out a longer, focused observation:

- Ensure you are clear about what, why and how you are observing.

- Be as unobtrusive as possible, the more observations you carry out the children will gradually become used to seeing you observe and are less likely to ask what you are doing.

- Avoid eye contact if possible with the child you are observing, so the child does not know they are being observed.

- Be aware of factors in the environment of the setting or in the child's own life that may affect their behaviour.

- Remember if a child knows that they are being observed, they may change their behaviour.

To be able to use your observations to provide you with relevant information, you need to ensure that your observations are accurate, of value and qualitative.

You are looking to build up a holistic view of the child, so you need a collection of observations of the child playing, on their own, interacting with others, indoors, outdoors, at meal and snack time, within a group e.g. story time. This needs to be achieved using a variety of observation methods, as different methods can provide you with different information. (These will be explained in the Observation Methods section). You need to ensure you remember that you are trying to record EVERYTHING and not just the child at play or engaged in an activity. Think about the value of observing children at the beginning or end of the day, when they might be tired, and the insight it will give you into their emotional security and their key attachments.

Most importantly **you need to ensure that your observations are objective and not subjective**, that you record just what you see and not what you think a child may be thinking or feeling. Consider these two simple examples:

Child A is standing in the corner, he is rubbing his eyes.

Child A is standing in the corner, he is tired and he is rubbing his eyes.

The first sentence is an observation, the second sentence is not an observation, as it states subjectively that child A is tired. Although his actions may indicate that he is tired, you don't know for sure that that is the reason he is rubbing his eyes. It can be difficult when you know a child well, and recognise that this is a normal non-verbal communication action that usually signifies tiredness, not to put that assumption in the observation. The danger is that by going into an observation thinking you know everything about a child, you might miss something vital and new. **If you interpret a child's actions whilst you are observing, you stop observing and are focusing on why a child did something instead of watching carefully to see what happens next.**

With observations, the information can be in the detail. You need to try to record how a child does something e.g. "She picked up the cup with her right hand". This detail can provide vital information; in the example above the extra detail provides information about both the child's hand preference and fine motor skills. It is also important not to describe a child as happy or excited or sad, as again these are all subjective opinions. You need to describe what the child is doing, that may imply or indicate these emotions. For example, whether the child was laughing, smiling, clapping hands, said something to indicate how they felt, was crying or perhaps stamping their feet. This recognition of emotions can give you an indication of the child's non-verbal communication skills as well as how a child expresses emotions and understands their own feelings.

Observations should be written in the present tense and describe something exactly as it happens.

Building up the whole picture of a child

So what can an observation tell you about a child?

The true value of observations is in the information that they provide you with, and then of course it is a question of how you use that information. This leads on from the first question looking at the reasons as to why observe children to what can observations tell you? Observations can provide information on all the areas covered in 'so why do we observe'. Basically, it will allow you to identify skills and understanding that a child may have shown, as well as demonstrate how a child's learning and development has progressed.

The Early Years Foundation Stage identifies five key skills for observations:

- **Looking:** understanding what you are looking for in terms of where the child is at and what you know about their development.

- **Listening:** taking note and listening to the interactions of the child with others and any verbal responses they may make.

- **Recording:** noting the important features of what you observe.

- **Thinking:** about and reflecting on what you have seen.

- **Questioning:** asking yourself questions about what you have seen to help your understanding and interpretation. This can be found on the (archived) National Strategies' CD-Rom *Observation, Assessment and Planning: Effective Practice*.

That is what the EYFS asks you to do to show not only that you are observing the children, but that you are also using that information to support their progress through the seven areas of learning and development, and providing appropriate experiences for them. You need to demonstrate direct links between your

The skill of writing observations in this way helps to prevent you from writing what you think or including subjective assumptions. Below are two examples of recording exactly what you see:

"Child D moves the middle finger of her right hand backwards and forwards in the spilt milk, she then moves her finger to the right and then moves back to the left."

"Child C holds the paintbrush in the palm of his right hand, *his fingers are curled round the brush, moving his arm forward he stabs the paintbrush on the paper."*

You need to always approach observations from a position of enquiry, asking ourselves questions about the child as we reflect. What have I learnt about this child? What do I now know that I didn't know before about the child? What is the child telling me? What exactly is the child doing or saying?

observations, the experiences provided for the children and your planning.

It is about taking the information from the observations and using it appropriately. In the DCSF (2009) document *Learning, Playing and Interacting* it states:

> *'The adult is an interested observer of play, finding out about the individual child and the community that is created through play. The adult should seek to discover what children are interested in, know and can do in order to support their learning more effectively. Children's achievements across all areas of learning can be recognised through observing play.'*

The importance of effective planning

Planning needs to be spontaneous and flexible and responsive to children. If you approach your planning with this attitude it will have meaning and context for the children. If children can learn in a context appropriate to them, whether that is in relation to an interest they may have or something within or just beyond their realm of experience, they will gain much more from the experience.

Again you need to consider why planning is so important. It can be seen as a time-consuming chore, but it does have an essential purpose and being aware of that can help the process.

So why do you need to plan?

- For organisation within the setting, to ensure you know what you are doing and have the necessary resources available.

- To ensure you are providing a broad and balanced experience for children through a variety of opportunities, both indoors and outdoors.

- To enable you to meet children's individual needs, by reflecting on what you know about the children and what you identify through observations in your planning.

- To promote learning and development, by meeting children's individual needs.

- To ensure you are providing appropriate challenges for the children and supporting their active learning.

- To introduce new ideas and experiences.

- To help you provide for any gaps in children's experience and learning.

- To inform other professionals and parents, so that they can share in the children's discoveries and experiences.

Planning helps you to ensure that you are providing the best opportunities for the children. You need however to give careful consideration to how children learn as this needs to be reflected in your planning. The principles of the 'A Unique Child' theme in the EYFS is:

> *'Every child is a unique child who is constantly learning and can be resilient, capable, confident and self-assured.'*

It is essential that you understand and recognise this and utilise every opportunity to promote learning. In the DCSF document *Learning, Playing and Interacting – Good Practice in the Early Years Foundation Stage*, it states that:

> *'Young children are not passive learners ... they actively drive their own learning and development by the choices they make, the interests they develop, the questions they ask, the knowledge they seek and their motivation to act more competently.'*

This needs to be reflected in the choices that you offer and the opportunities and experiences you provide within the setting.

You should also remember and consider the following key points taken from *First Things First: Educating Young Children. A Guide for Parents and Governors* (1992):

> *"Children learn most effectively by doing rather than being told."*
> *"Children learn most effectively when they are actively involved and interested."*

So how do children learn?

- Through play – this is how they make sense of the world and make discoveries.

- Through challenges, both physical and mental. An appropriate and achievable challenge provides stimulation, fuels the imagination and problem solving skills and develops concentration and absorption.

- Through repetition – children need to revisit experiences to hone skills and to consolidate understanding; this is why they need to see the same or similar opportunities available in the continuous provision.

- Through imitation and copying others – children may learn through watching an adult or a more experienced peer, and imitate this in their role play which helps to develop their own understanding of their world.

- Being active – if children make choices and direct their own learning, they are more actively involved and engaged with the experience and will learn more.

- Through trial and error – trying again and again or different ways of doing something to get there in the end.

- Through exploration, investigation and experimentation – feeding on their natural curiosity to find things out, using their senses to aid understanding.

- Explaining – talking through their ideas, or talking through a problem, can help clarity and understanding.

You can't just provide these opportunities and hope for the best. You need to know that children have learnt something new from the experience. You can make a judgment on each child's learning through your observations and assessments, by monitoring their progress and skill development. You may also see transference of skills, where a child uses a skill learnt in one area somewhere else.

You need to know that children have learnt so you know that what you are providing is appropriate, you know they are stimulated, making progress and are developing.

The learning environment that you provide needs to facilitate the myriad of different learning intelligences that children have, so different combinations can be made by the individual and so they all have opportunity to explore, develop and learn. You need to ensure that children's learning environment provides these opportunities through:

- Reflecting each child's social and cultural background.

- Encouraging equality of opportunity.

- Valuing and building on previous experiences that each child has had, so they can direct their own learning to move forward.

- Providing resources and experiences that are accessible and open-ended.

- Giving opportunity for first-hand experiences, letting children explore and investigate.

- Allow children the freedom and space to explore.

- Develop confidence and self esteem.

- Allow for the development and understanding of ideas and knowledge.

- Allow time for children to assimilate their experiences.

- Promote independence and autonomy.

- Allow for continuity of play, ensure you support free flow play.

- Allow for a variety of learning situations.

- Encourage the development of skills and attitudes.

- Foster social relationships.

- Encourage communication, both verbal and non-verbal.

- Allow the child time for solitary activity.

- Develop positive attitudes to learning through self-initiated activity and decision making.

- Motivate the child to learn.

- Allow for the development of the process skills involved in experiential learning.

- Ensuring an appropriate balance of child-initiated and adult-led experiences.

The practice guide for the Enabling Enviornments theme in the EYFS states that the enabling environment should offer:

'Stimulating resources, relevant to all the children's cultures and communities

Ensure the learning environment provides opportunities to explore, develop and learn

through play and playful teaching, support for children to take risks and explore.'

Delivering an enabling environment is about setting the scene and facilitating learning for all.

A regular audit and review of your learning environment, both indoors and outdoors, will help ensure that your provision is developing as the children are, and developing to meet their needs. Effective planning and observations will contribute to this process and give you clues as to the appropriateness of what you are providing both indoors and outdoors. For example, a practitioner noticed that rather than using the new stepping stone path, children were more interested in the grassy mound that had been created in the centre, and enjoyed rolling up and down the hill. From this observation, it was decided to put steps in the hill so that the younger children could also enjoy this activity.

Remember though that your observations can only be as good as the learning environment in which they take place.

Observations and planning can be used not simply to tell you about the individual child, but also about your provision. You can also carry out observations e.g. a time sample (explained in the 'Observation methods' section) on a particular resource or item of equipment to see how or if the children are using the resource. This is particularly useful if you feel play has stagnated or you don't think the children are using a particular resource.

The emotional environment

Development and learning will only be effective though if the children are happy and safe. This is where the emotional environment comes in. The emotional environment is about ensuring the children feel settled

Exploring natural resources

Key points to remember when planning the outdoor environment

- You need to reflect a balance of child-initiated and adult-led experiences outdoors.

- Don't simply take indoor resources outside, or have the same resources outdoors as indoors. Think about how you can provide something different outside, e.g. construction materials indoors might include Duplo, Stickle bricks, whereas outdoors they might include cardboard boxes and crates for construction as you may have more space, and play can be more realistic and open-ended.

- Try to create areas outside to make it more appealing to children, just as you would inside, use bamboo screening or drape curtains from washing lines.

- If all the rooms in a day nursery share the same outdoor space, plan together so you can identify resources that can be made available across the age ranges, to prevent constantly having to change the provision completely.

- Ensure through your observations that you identify those children whose learning appears to be accelerated outside.

- Consider sensory exploration and stimulation when planning the outdoor environment.

- If you have no outdoor area, ensure that you make use of your local area e.g. green spaces, parks, going for walks, going to shops, posting a letter.

and secure in order for learning and development to flourish. Without this sense of security children will not feel able to do all they need to move on and progress.

The below list encompasses a variety of strategies that focus on establishing the feeling of emotional security in your setting.

- Home visits show not only that you value the child, but that you are interested in them and their family and this can help break down barriers in approaching the child's parents/carers.

- Establishing a key person system.

- A key carer who knows their key children's special words and understands their routines.

- A personalised settling in process.

- 'All about me' established starting points (see the accompanying CD-Rom for more on this).

- Reflecting the child's home and background in the setting.

- Good relationships between parents and the setting.

- Named pegs, drawers or their own space to keep things.

- A familiar environment with recognisable resources.

- Adults who have realistic expectations of them.

- Quiet places to go in the setting.

- Children's likes and interests are reflected in the provision.

- Children know they are liked, accepted and will be listened to.

- Children feel that the setting is a place where they can express their feelings and emotions.

- Children feel that the setting is a place where they are nurtured, cared for and loved.

The adult plays a crucial and critical role in establishing this emotional environment. Practitioners' ability to establish this sense of security for children is strengthened through the relationships they build with the children, the environment they provide and the observations they carry out.

The commitment card 2.3 in the Early Years Foundation Stage pack (2007) states that:

"*Effective practitioners observe children sensitively and respond appropriately to encourage and extend curiosity and learning.*"

"*By observing and listening, the [practitioner] discovers what children like to do and when they feel scared or frustrated.*"

You need to ensure your setting has clearly defined areas that are organised with accessible resources that are clearly labelled with both the written name and picture if appropriate. This creates a sense of interest to the children and invites children's natural inquisitiveness.

Once the scene is set, the starting points have been established and you feel you have a clear understanding of the importance and value of observations and planning you can begin with confidence to engage in effective observations and planning.

The setting is a place where the children are nurtured, cared for and loved

Good practice checklist for observations

☐ Have a schedule for focused observations, so they become part of everyday practice and to ensure some children are not overlooked.

☐ Observe children in different areas and at different times, using various observation methods to build up a holistic picture of the child.

☐ Carry out very brief anecdotal or spontaneous observations.

☐ Remember observations are useful in evaluating the provision.

☐ Be clear about what you are looking for and why in focused observations.

☐ Regular and frequent observations give a greater understanding of individual children.

☐ Approach observations from a position of enquiry rather than judgment, asking yourself "What can I learn about this child?", "What is the child telling me?", or "What do I now know that I didn't know before?"

☐ Record exactly what you see not what you think or assume you see; be objective, not subjective.

☐ Use descriptive language with enough detail to give a clear picture, don't say a child is happy or sad: describe what they do.

☐ Although key carers observe their key children, it can be good occasionally for another practitioner to observe a child as they may pick up on something new. This can be especially helpful if you have a concern about a child.

☐ Interpret or analyse observations, ask yourself "What exactly is the child doing or saying?" and "What do I understand from this?"

☐ Provide sensitive interpretations avoiding judgmental language.

☐ Ask "How might I build on this interest?" or "How could I present that experience more attractively, to make it more appealing?"

☐ Ensure you show links on your observations to the EYFS.

☐ Ensure you identify next steps on your observations and that these are reflected in your planning.

☐ Invite parents/guardians to contribute to children's observations.

Good practice checklist for planning

☐ Ensure that the whole team is involved in planning.

☐ Planning needs to be responsive to children and not planned weeks in advance.

☐ Allow yourself to be flexible and spontaneous in your planning.

☐ Activities and experiences need to take place in a meaningful context for children.

☐ Reflect children's likes and interests in planning.

☐ Annotate your plans to show when something has been changed in response to children.

☐ Involve the children in planning, listen to their ideas.

☐ Ensure you provide a wide variety of activities and experiences and reflect the seven areas of learning and development.

☐ Ensure your planning supports the different ways in which children learn.

☐ Provide a balance of child-initiated and adult-led experiences, both indoors and outdoors.

☐ Ensure you show clear links on your planning to observations of children.

☐ Share your planning with parents.

☐ Ensure that anyone visiting your setting can see how the planning cycle works for individual children.

☐ Be flexible in your planning. Don't be afraid to let go of what you have planned if it isn't working, or if something unforeseen happens that interests the children.

Observation methods

Using a variety of different methods of observation will help you to build up a holistic picture of each child and what stage of development he or she is at. Some methods are more suited to different circumstances and situations and we will discuss this in this section.

Tips for getting started:

- Firstly, you must have the parent's or guardian's consent to make written observations of their children. Obviously it is in the child's best interests that observations are carried out and recorded, so if a parent is reluctant to give consent you would need to explain the benefits to the child, emphasising that observations are confidential.

- You need to be organised and prepared – these can be two completely separate things. You'll need to be prepared to make snapshot observations for which you'll need some sticky notes and a pen with you at all times. But you will also need to be ready to take out more lengthy planned observations, and for this you'll need to have printed off observation forms ready and have prepared for some time out to carry out the observation.

- To gain a truly holistic view of the child you will need to plan when to carry out some observations, some can be random to give a view of what the child accesses and enjoys but others may need to be of planned activities to observe certain skills. You need to use a range of observations and a range of times and activities both indoors and outdoors.

- In some settings the person observing is recognisable by wearing a sash or a crown so that other staff and children know what they are doing and can avoid interrupting them.

- You will need to be flexible – you may have planned to observe a child playing in the sand and the child doesn't go near the sand, so you have to decide whether to observe on a different day or on a different activity.

- Before you start you need to know what the aim of the observation is – what do you want to find out? For example are you looking at a particular area of development? This will help you to determine the type and timing of the observation and allow you to be focused without being prejudiced. Even when doing snapshot observations it is important to know why you're doing them or you just end up with lots of sticky notes that don't really tell you very much. I once saw a sticky note observation that said "TC picked up a blue brick". That was it, nothing else. At the time it was written it may have meant something, but to me reading it later it didn't have much meaning at all. I didn't know if he'd been asked to pick up a blue brick, I didn't know which hand he'd picked it up in as nothing was explained, so the observation lacked essential detail and as such failed to have any value.

- You need to decide if you wish the child to be aware that they are being observed. Children need to be involved in observations, but we all know that we behave differently when we are aware that we're being watched so sometimes it is best to be unobtrusive. This

It is important to sit back and observe how a child engages with a resource

Involve other people in your observations

of course doesn't mean that you can't share the observation with the child afterwards.

■ Involve other people in your observations – this may only be to the extent of telling other members of staff what you are doing so they can give you the time and space that you need. It is important to remember that no-one can observe everything and others may have seen something that you haven't, or have a different perspective on it that you hadn't considered. You can ask parents to be involved by carrying out further observations at home or simply telling you face to face how the child is at home. Each child should have been observed by more than their key person when putting together the EYFS profile, as one person alone cannot possibly know the full picture of any child.

■ When you are writing your observation in the first instant,

spelling and grammar aren't important as long as you can understand what you mean. If you are worried about spelling and grammar it is best to type them up on a computer if you have access to one and use the spell check to spot any errors. It is important when parents and carers are reading your observations that they are spelt correctly because you are responsible for educating their children.

■ On your more lengthy observations you need to identify the next steps for the child. That is to say what you think the child should do next to enhance their development. You must be extremely careful here, as children do not respond well to being target driven. Development is a fluid process so the next step must be a natural progression and a working knowledge of child development will be necessary in order to determine this. A way of sharing this information with all staff

is to have a poster positioned away from public view that identifies what next steps are suggested for each child. That way any practitioner can be aware and focus on these next steps if they get the opportunity.

■ Discuss observations through with parents and children, adding their comments after the observation.

When you are ready to carry out the observation be focused and try to forget everything that you previously knew about the child. Imagine you have just met them and it is like working on a blank canvas. This should make it easier to be factual – for example if you have any preconceived ideas that can influence what you see and affect accuracy. When you come to evaluate it is time to take what you already know into account but during the observation only write what you see. Don't assume a child is enjoying an activity because they are smiling: the observation should just state that they are smiling. However, do take careful note of their body language and non-verbal communication, as this will inform you of their likes and dislikes. You may also note their physical wellbeing. Don't assume because a child is yawning that they are tired, simply write that they are yawning – it may be that the child is bored!

Snapshot observations

In order to start snapshot observations you will need sticky notes and a pen.

A snapshot observation, also called a 'surprise and delight observation' is quite literally what it sounds like – it provides an instant picture of what is happening there and then. To be useful it must be dated and linked to the EYFS or early years curricula you work with. On some snapshot observations you will want to record the next steps for the child, but this isn't normally necessary on every single one. It is always good to see practitioners around with their sticky notes carrying out lots of snapshot observations, but they must only be seen as a start.

Advantages

- Snapshot observations are quick and easy to do.

Disadvantages

- Because they are quick and easy to do sometimes they are the only kind of observations that are carried out.

- They are difficult to evaluate because they contain a limited amount of information, this makes it difficult to use these observations in order to build up a child's profile.

- You have to read through a lot of them to gain a real picture of the child.

- As snapshot observations are done randomly, and in an unplanned way, it is difficult to make sure that all areas are being observed.

- They are easily lost.

Spontaneous observations

Spontaneous observations are observations that are somewhere between sticky notes and a full narrative observation, and provide a full snapshot of the child at a given moment. They can take the form of photographs, for example. They need to be linked to the EYFS and identify the next steps for the child.

What you will need

A proforma – two observations can fit on one A4 sheet of paper. There is no need for a front sheet as all the details necessary are on the proforma.

What to do

Simply record the child's name, date of birth and the date. Then write down what the child is doing – or paste in a photograph of what the child is doing, but this needs to be annotated because a photo can be very open-ended.

Then write down any links to the EYFS – for example if a child has successfully caught a large ball through developed co-ordination, link this to the Physical Development area of learning and development, moving and handling 30-50 months 'can catch a large ball.'

Following this, write down the next steps that you consider important for this child – this may be to develop or consolidate that activity or to move on to a related one. With the catching a ball example above you may decide that the next step is for the child to try to catch a smaller ball.

Advantages

- Spontaneous observations are not time-consuming; they can also provide significant information succinctly.

- Anyone can do a spontaneous observation: they are a good place to start for building practitioner's confidence and skills.

Disadvantages

- There is a risk of having a pile of sticky notes, which you do nothing with in terms of follow up

as they make no sense to you at a later stage.

- You can end up recording things that aren't relevant.

Narrative observations

Narrative observations consist of the observer writing down everything that a child says and does. It forms a detailed picture of the child. With narrative observation there is the potential of having an awful lot to note down, and choices will need to be made about what to include. A way to do this is to decide what aspect of the child's play or development you want to focus on.

*A **snapshot** observation provides an instant picture of what is happening there and then*

A narrative observation should be between 10 and 20 minutes in duration, as any longer and the value of information could be compromised, as the observer will be fatigued from the intense concentration.

What you will need

All you will need in order to carry out a narrative observation is a front sheet, some blank paper and a pen or pencil and something to lean on.

What to do

Start by describing the context on the front sheet, for example include where the child is playing and if other children are present.

Write down what you see and hear as you see it. Ensure you include other children's responses as well. You need to write in the present tense and you will need to record accurately what the child says because observations are used for evidence if you are calling in other professionals if you believe the child needs further help. So if a child says, "Pass me the dar", meaning pass me the car, then you must write the former, as that is what you heard. Please be aware that this doesn't mean if a child says 'dar' instead of 'car' he will need speech therapy, it is simply a part of the jigsaw that builds up a picture of the child and if there are other issues it may be indicative of a problem.

You will also need to record adults or other children that speak during the observation and exactly what they say.

If you need to stop the observation or pause for any reason you need to record the time you stopped and the time you restarted.

As soon as possible after you have completed the observation you need to type or write it up neatly – unless you are super neat it is impossible to take everything down perfectly whilst observing the child. Then you need to draw conclusions from the observation. It is very important here that you only draw conclusions from what you have written down and not what you think you saw or you think the child can do based on preconceived ideas.

When drawing conclusions from any observation you need to consider what it means for the child being observed and how the information relates to theories of child development and links with the EYFS, and using all of that information consider how best to move the child on to the natural next steps.

To carry out a narrative observation most effectively it is best to be a non-participant, as you cannot write down your own responses.

Advantages

■ This method of observation is simple to use, and can provide a good snapshot of the child.

■ It is an open method of observation, which means that it provides a pool of information, and if done well gives a very full picture of the child.

■ Narrative observations can be spontaneous because they don't require any special tables of charts to complete it.

Disadvantages

■ However, it is difficult to record all of the information and to decide what to record and what to omit. It is also easy to miss something vital whilst you are writing down something else. It can be very frustrating when this happens.

■ In narrative observations you have to position yourself close to the child to pick up what they are saying, and this risks causing the child's behaviour to change.

■ Narrative observation is the most likely to be interrupted by other children, usually wanting to know what you are writing.

■ Narrative observation is a very subjective method: two people observing the same child for the

Narrative observation forms a detailed picture of the child

same period of time will record very different things because the observer is constantly making decisions about what is important to record.

- It is also a very tiring method of observing.

Tracking observations

Tracking observations are very similar to spider's web observations but aren't recorded in the presence of the parent. Tracking observations record where a child has been and how long they stayed there. The great advantage of tracking observations is that additional information can be added. For example, if an adult was present at an activity or if other children were present. Tracking observations can also be stopped at any time if something of interest happens, and a different sort of observation started. For example, if a child stays for 10 minutes at the water tray you may decide to carry out a narrative observation there.

Tracking observations can be used for a variety of purposes depending on the frequency and focus of your observations. Carrying out tracker observations repeatedly over a period of time will help develop a better understanding of an individual child's preferred activities. If you carry out tracker observations on several children and compare your observations this will allow you to evaluate the environment, to see whether any adjustments need to be made. For example, if it is noted that no children are accessing the sand or water play then you need to consider how those areas are presented: are they accessible, are there appropriate tools to play with in each area, and are they situated in the most convenient place, or would it be better if it was moved.

What you will need

Before you start you will need a simple diagram of your setting – you can include the outside area as well, or

you can approach this separately. On the diagram you need to show the activities that are available and their position in the room.

What to do

1. Start where the child is and draw an arrow to the first place that they move to. Put a number one midway along this arrow.

2. Note how long the child stays at the new activity and write this at the activity, e.g. five minutes.

3. If an adult is at the activity write the letter 'A' in a circle on the activity to indicate their presence.

4. Repeat this each time the child moves from one activity to another, timing how long they stay at each.

5. This observation can carry on for the duration of the session, or for any intervals you feel might be appropriate e.g. 30 minutes at a time.

6. When you have completed this you need to analyse what you have found out by asking yourself the following questions:

   Where did the child go?

   Where didn't the child go?

   Did the child repeatedly return to any activities?

   How long did the child stay at activities?

   What was the longest amount of time the child remained at an activity?

   Can you think of any reasons for or draw any conclusions from the above?

Using the completed tracker observation you could make the following statements and conclusions:

- The child visited the puzzles, the role-play area, the home corner and the play dough. They also visited the toilet, and briefly visited the train sets.

- The child didn't visit the sand or the water. Nor did they visit the books, the craft table, the construction or number activities, or the climbing frame.

- The child repeatedly returned to the home corner and stayed there for a fairly long duration.

- On average the child stayed at activities for a sustained period of time of up to 10 minutes.

- The longest time they stayed at an activity was 12 minutes at the play dough table. I would question whether this was because an adult was there, encouraging the child to stay for longer and engaging the child in conversation and activity.

- The child didn't access resources on one side of the room and I would need to investigate why this might be. It could be the layout of these activities, the fact that the staff were not encouraging the child to go to them, they were noisier and bigger activities and may therefore pose a threat to this child. I would need to do several tracker observations to collect the information that I need.

Advantages

Tracker observations are an ideal observation to start with for both children and staff. Staff only need a limited amount of skill to carry out the observation and can be helped in their evaluation by the leader or another member of staff.

Staff also don't have to worry about writing masses of information down, checking their spelling or catching everything. A tracker observation can be made as simple as necessary, or you can add your own notes for further details.

A great advantage of tracker observations is that when the child spends a long time at the play dough table for example, the observer can then switch to a narrative observation, or alternatively plan to do the next narrative observation at the play dough table.

Another advantage of this type of observation is that the child doesn't need to be aware that you are observing them because the observation can be carried out from a distance, as it isn't necessary to record what a child says.

Disadvantages

It is difficult to draw accurate conclusions with the little information provided in a tracker observation. I could assume that the child stayed at the play dough table because an adult was there interacting with them and encouraging them, however this may not be the reason. Possibly the adult didn't talk to the child. There is no way of knowing from the information gathered. Looking at the completed observation the child rarely goes to an activity where there is an adult present (except for the play dough) – this could be because they are anxious about adults that they know less well than their key person. However, this information can't be drawn from this observation alone, further tracker observations would need to be repeated to see whether a pattern emerges.

Commonly asked questions

Q: What if a child never quite reaches an activity and simply hovers nearby looking at other children?

A: If this happens finish your arrow away from the activity and still record how long the child stayed observing.

Children can learn from observing their peers

If the child then moves on to the activity start a new arrow or put another head on the arrow.

Q: What if a child is running round and round and doesn't stop at an activity?

A: If this happens you would just draw your arrows going round and round and you wouldn't add timings as the child hasn't stopped – however you could time how long they run around for without stopping as everyone has to stop sometime!

Q: What other information can I add to a tracker observation?

A: The beauty of tracker observations is that you can add any information that you think you may need. You can add if an adult is at an activity, or if other children are there. You could write a note of why the child doesn't stay – for example the child may only have stayed at the trains for one minute because the other children wouldn't let him play or because no-one else was there.

Q: What if the child I am tracking stays in the same place and doesn't move?

A: This does not make the observation invalid: it could be an indication that the child is engaged in the activity or experience. Alternatively, it could indicate that they feel some sense of security where they are and are reluctant to move elsewhere. In this case it would be wise to do a further observation on a different day to give you some further clarification.

Event sampling

Event sampling can be used to focus on any of the following areas:

■ Potential patterns in children's behaviour, particularly unwanted behaviour, in order to try and identify the triggers for that behaviour.

■ Particular aspects of a child's activity – for example you may want to know if they are accessing malleable resources frequently.

■ To assess your own resources – e.g. record each time a child visits the sand to evaluate and see if you need to make adjustments to your provision.

Recording only happens in this type of observation when a particular behaviour is shown by the child – hence the term 'event'. For example, if you had a child in the setting who didn't often speak to an adult you would record only when they did speak to that adult. For these observations you need to begin by identifying what you need to know – i.e. what the 'event' will be. So, if you have a child who bites, the 'event' is whenever that child bites someone. In order to take an event sample you also need to identify what you need to know so that you know what to record. For example, you may need to know the time it happens, is it when the child is tired or hungry? You may want to know the social grouping the child is in at the time – is it when they are in a large group and fighting for attention? For everything you need to know you will need a specific column to record the information, it is also useful to have a spare column for comments.

What you will need

You will need to prepare a chart for recording in advance with the necessary number of columns. An example of a chart is available on page 24.

You may well need more than one observer for this observation – whoever sees the behaviour should be the one to record it, so all practitioners need to be aware of the observation. See the time sample observation form on page 23.

Advantages

■ This observation requires the observer to take on the role of a detective and is a useful way of finding out about a child, or about activities that you provide for children.

Disadvantages

■ The prepared sheet needs to have been very carefully thought out or the observation will not work.

Characteristics of effective learning

The Characteristics of Effective Learning underpin your practice and support the children's learning across all the areas of learning and development. All practitioners need to have a clear understanding of the three characteristics:

■ **Playing and Exploring** – engagement.

■ **Active Learning** – motivation.

■ **Creating and Thinking Critically** – thinking.

what they mean in practice and how to support children. These characteristics have been linked to three of the themes of the Early Years Foundation Stage.

The 'A Unique Child' theme is asking you to think how you provide the experiences and opportunities linked to the characteristics for the child to be involved through their own choice and decision. For example consider how provide for children to seek challenge, pay attention to detail, engage in open ended activity and think of ideas.

Positive Relationships is about how you might support the child to learn in relation to the characteristics and Enabling Environments is about what you provide to support the facilitation of the characteristics of effective learning.

These characteristics all strongly support independence and child-initiated learning in an environment that includes both the indoors and outdoors and is flexible and supportive and encourages first hand experience. An environment where the adult sensitively intervenes to support learning and may plan activities accordingly.

The characteristics as described on pages 7 and 8 of the 'Development Matters' document (2012) are excellent tools for reflective practice and reviewing the learning environment.

Targeted child observations can provide a wealth of information

The characteristics of effective learning – A Unique Child

With the 'A Unique Child' theme it is suggested you observe children learning in different styles related to the characteristics. To do this, you need to ensure appropriate opportunities are available to the children. This chart is designed to help you consider and reflect on the appropriateness of your provision.

PLAYING AND EXPLORING engagement	Learning opportunity	Examples	Ways in which this is enabled in your setting	How could it be developed and improved
	FINDING OUT AND EXPLORING ■ Showing curiosity about objects, events and people. ■ Using senses to explore the world around them. ■ Engaging in open-ended activity. ■ Showing particular interests.			
	PLAYING WITH WHAT THEY KNOW ■ Pretending objects are things from their experience. ■ Representing their experiences in play. ■ Taking on a role in their play. ■ Acting out experiences with other people.			
	BEING WILLING TO HAVE A GO ■ Initiating activities. ■ Seeking challenge. ■ Showing a 'can do' attitude. ■ Taking a risk, engaging in new experiences, and learning by trial and error.			
ACTIVE LEARNING motivation	Learning opportunity	Examples	Ways in which this is enabled in your setting	How could it be developed and improved
	BEING INVOLVED AND CONCENTRATING ■ Maintain focus on their activity for a period of time. ■ Showing high levels of energy, fascination. ■ Not easily distracted. ■ Paying attention to details.			

ACTIVE LEARNING	Learning opportunity	Examples	Ways in which this is enabled in your setting	How could it be developed and improved
motivation	KEEP ON TRYING ■ Persisting with the activity when challenges occur. ■ Showing a belief that more effort or a different approach will pay off. ■ Bouncing back after difficulties.			
	ENJOYING AND ACHIEVING WHAT THEY SET OUT TO DO ■ Showing satisfaction in meeting their own goals. ■ Being proud of how they accomplished something – not just the end result. ■ Enjoying meeting challenges for their own sake rather than external rewards or praise.			
CREATING AND THINKING CRITICALLY	Learning opportunity	Examples	Ways in which this is enabled in your setting	How could it be developed and improved
thinking	HAVING THEIR OWN IDEAS ■ Thinking of ideas. ■ Finding ways to solve problems. ■ Finding new ways to do things.			
	MAKING LINKS ■ Making links and noticing patterns in their experience. ■ Making predictions. ■ Testing their ideas. ■ Developing ideas of grouping, sequences, cause and effect.			
	CHOOSING WAYS TO DO THINGS ■ Planning, making decisions about how to approach a task, solve a problem and reach a goal. ■ Checking how well their activities are going. ■ Changing strategy as needed. ■ Reviewing how well the approach worked.			

An example of a tracker observation

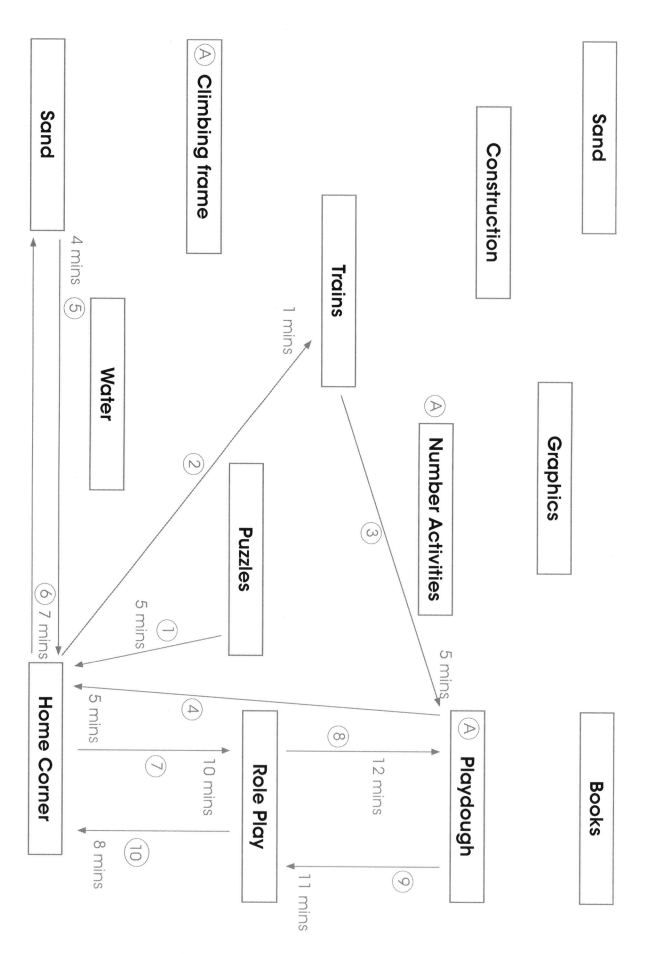

Child's name: Ben   **Date:** 12th May 2010   **Date of birth:** 24th Jan 2007

Aim of observation: to identify how this child spends his time in the pre-school setting. Observe for duration of one minute at five-minute intervals.

Time	What the child is doing	Social group	Comments
9.15	At the play dough table involved in making the play dough	Adult and four children	Child is carefully scooping the flour into a cup for measuring
9.20	Rolling play dough out into a sausage shape	Six children	
9.25	Using play dough in the home corner. Pretending to cook with bun tins	One other child	Accurate use of representation
9.30	Dressing up in a fairy costume in the home corner	Solitary play	
9.35	Dancing around the room still wearing fairy costume	Group play	Adult has put on some music
9.40	At snack bar – has chosen banana and pita bread. Drinking water	Adult and two other children	
9.45	Still at snack table, says to adult "I've finished now"	Adult and two other children	
9.50	Washing hands in cloakroom	Solitary	
9.55	In outside role play area building a den with blocks and material	Co-operatively with three other children	

Links to the EYFS

PSED: self confidence and self awareness, 30–50 months. Can select and use activities and resources.

EAD: being imaginative 30-50 months. Uses available resources to create props to support role play. This links into the playing and exploring characteristics of effective learning.

Evaluation

Ben has a positive approach to activities and experiences as he moves freely around the room and outdoors making choices as to what he wishes to do. He displays symbolic play in using the play dough to represent the cakes in the home corner demonstrating free flow play. He can independently look after his own needs by choosing when to go to the snack bar, choosing what to eat and when to go and wash his hands. He displays an obvious interest in imaginative play through the play dough, the home corner, dressing up and outside role play. He is happy to engage in activities both by himself and co-operatively with other children and adults. He has the ability to make choices and direct his own learning.

Next steps

- Simple cooking activities where children can measure the ingredients.
- Additions to the learning environment.
- Develop outside dressing up resources to support role play area.
- Add a variety of kitchen utensils to home corner.

An example event sample chart

Event	Time and date	Situation	Social group	Comment	Dialogue
TC bit HC on the arm	9.15 am 30.04.10	Mat time and registration	Large group of children	Mat time had been going on for 15 minutes with a group of 24 children	HC to TC: "It's not your turn" when HC wanted to show his toy boat
TC hit AD on the face	10.30 am 30.04.10	Snack time – sitting round the table	TC and four other children	Children were pouring their own drinks with adult supervision. AD had spilt his drink and didn't want to mop it up. TC said "Naughty boy" and hit him	AD to TC: "Naughty boy"
TC bit DG on the arm	12.22 pm 01.05.10	Home time	Most children have been collected – TC on mat on his own until DG came over to him	DG was teasing TC that his mummy hadn't come to collect him because he was a naughty boy	DG to TC: "Your mummy isn't coming to get you because you are a naughty boy and you bite people"

What the child did	Inappropriate next step	Why it is inappropriate	Appropriate next step	Why it is appropriate
Child is sitting at the snack table moving their middle finger backwards and forwards and in a circular motion in spilt milk	Sand play or water play	The child is engaging in an enjoyable tactile experience, they are discovering they can make marks. Sand and water play, whilst tactile, don't support the discovery of mark making or enable the child to see the results of mark making	Corn flour or finger painting	Corn flour and finger painting are both tactile experiences and support the discovery of mark making using fingers. It is this activity that has fascinated and interested the child, so that is what you need to build on in the next step
A child is knocking two plastic trains together, looks at them as they make a noise and then moves to tap them on a table top	Play musical instruments	The child is enjoying the discovery that he can make a noise with the trains, musical instruments will definitely make a noise but there is no element of discovery for the child	Providing different surfaces for the child to bang the trains on or other objects that can be used to make a noise	The child has then got the opportunity to explore and discover what other noises he can make with the trains or with other objects for himself, using open-ended resources
A child runs outside, pushes their hands and arms into a pile of leaves, and scoops them up into the air	Make a collage with leaves	The child is enjoying the outside physical enjoyment of engaging with the leaves and discovering what they can do. Making a collage with the leaves is not exploring this interest with the child	Repeat by using tools to re-pile leaves parachute	This is an extension of the engagement with the leaves and developing an interest in their properties and other natural objects
A child is using scissors to snip into a piece of paper	Cutting out a square or other pre-drawn shape	This is way beyond the child's developmental capability and serves no purpose. The child needs to develop their fine motor and manipulative skills, alongside their scissor skills	Provide different types of paper, straws and material for the child to snip	This experience will develop the child's scissor skills and build their confidence
A child is struggling to hold a short stubby paintbrush	Provide a long thin paintbrush or crayons	The child needs to develop their manipulative skills and muscle control to be able to hold the paintbrush successfully, this will not be supported by providing other awkward objects for them to manipulate	Bead threading, sponge painting. Painting with large household brushes, or using play dough	These activities all support development of manipulative skills and muscle control
A child counts by rote from 1 to 20	To recognise numerals visually up to 20	The child can say the numbers but this does not mean that they can recognise numerical figures. Recognising numbers is a completely different skill and requires different understanding to counting	To count out a specific amount of something, for example say to the child "Could you count out four cars on to the table top?"	Although it was observed that the child could count, the observer was unsure as to whether the child could appreciate the quantative value of a number

Spontaneous observation record sheet

Date: 14th May 2010

Child's name: Child A

Date of birth: 15th January 2009

What I saw: Child A is sitting at the snack table. The child places both hands down flat on the tabletop. She lifts her right hand up and moves it back down and forward in some spilt milk on the table. She then lifts her hand up again and uses the middle finger of her right hand and moves it backwards and forwards in the milk and round and round in an anticlockwise circle.

Links to the EYFS:

PD: moving and handling, 8-20 months – enjoys the sensory experience of making marks in damp sand, paste of paint.

Characteristics of Effective Learning: play and exploring.

Next steps: Corn flour and finger painting.

Date:

Child's name:

Date of birth:

What I saw:

Links to the EYFS:

Next steps:

Child's Name: Ella

Age: 3 years 6 months

Date of Birth: 01.12.2006

Key carer: Jane

Time of observation: 1.45pm

Date: 13th May 2010

Setting: Indoor home corner

Aim of observation: To identify Ella's language skills in role play.

Observation: Ella is standing by the telephone; she turns to another child and asks, "What is your phone number?" Child A replies "H, J, K, L, M, N, O, P, Q, T". Ella turns to look at child A and frowns, and then using the first finger of her right hand she taps out the phone number, stabbing each number. Ella then picks up the receiver in her right hand and lifts it to her ear, says "Hello" then pauses and turns to Child A holding out the receiver whilst saying, "It's your Mum". Child A takes the phone; Ella sits down on the chair by the telephone, saying "Now my phone number". Child A replies, "What is your phone number?" Ella replies "I know it is 0811 366 7089". Child A gives her the receiver, Ella takes it in her right hand and lifts it to her ear saying "Hello Mummy", she then pauses … "Ok, yeah, yeah". Ella then puts down the receiver and moves away.

Links to the EYFS:

CL: speaking, 30-50 months, builds up vocabulary that reflects the breadth of their experience.

PSED: making relationships, 30-50 months, can play in a group extending and elaborating play ideas.

EAD: being imaginative, 30-50 months, engages in imaginative play and role play based on own first hand experiences.

Evaluation: Ella has displayed language skills that reflect observations she has made of everyday life, she is able to lead the role play interaction and has demonstrated a clear and appropriate use of language. Additionally she has shown an ability to control language in a special and complex way, particularly in only responding non-verbally when her friend uses letters for her number instead of numbers. Perhaps she was respecting some unspoken rule over imaginative speech in role play. Ella shows an understanding of numbers in appropriate context as she relates her 'phone number' and is a clearly confident in taking turns in conversation both real and imagined.

Next Steps:

Learning environment: Add mark making materials and telephone directories to the home corner.
IMMEDIATE ACTION.

Adult-led experience: Use a dictaphone for the children to record themselves talking, and then listen back to the tape. Children shouldn't be aware that they are being recorded. So they are not inhibited in their talk. Use as a point of discussion when listening back to the tape.

All about planning

There are seven areas of learning and development in the EYFS. There are three **prime** areas which are Personal, Social and Emotional Development, Communication and Language and Physical Development. These provide the basis for successful learning and development.

There are four **specific** areas: Literacy, Mathematics, Understanding the World and Expressive Arts and Design. The specific areas evolve out of the prime areas as a natural progression.

Practitioners working with the youngest children will focus primarily on the prime areas, which is reflected in the 'Development Matters' document. If at any point you have any concern about a child's progress in any of the three prime areas, you need to discuss with the child's parents how you are going to work together to support the child.

Good planning is the key to making children's learning effective, exciting, varied and progressive.

This is really powerful language and it demonstrates that planning is essential: without it learning may not happen effectively and children cannot progress. The Early Years Foundation Stage guidance also states that planning "enables practitioners to build up knowledge about how individual children learn and make progress". So, good and effective planning will need to be coupled with accurate observations on the children and the environment.

We have all heard of the well know idiom 'fail to plan, plan to fail', and it is in fact true: every area of provision needs to be planned for in some form or another. To be able to plan effectively we need to know what we want to get out of the activity or area. **The most important thing is that plans are flexible within them to respond to children's interests and needs and therefore you need to be willing to let go of your plans at a moment's notice and go with the flow.**

The most important thing is that plans are flexible to respond to children's interests and needs

Sometimes it is through over-planning that inflexibility occurs, meaning that practitioners can't be spontaneous and responsive to the children because they are so concerned with getting through every activity they have planned that there is no time to expand on individual activities or respond to what the children are interested in. If a child brings a caterpillar into the setting you have to be able to respond to that; perhaps by reading *The Very Hungry Caterpillar* (Puffin, 1994) or making the caterpillar an appropriate home – and leave your plan to make daffodils that day. **It is far more important that children are interested, stimulated and learning, than that you are sticking to your plans.** When you divert from your plans simply annotating on your plans is sufficient – don't be afraid to scribble on your plans and make them look messy, this is good practice.

Planning will take a different form in every setting (in order to respond to the type of setting, the children attending etc.) and this is why the EYFS doesn't provide set planning formats. **Whatever format your planning takes you must leave space in it to be able respond to children's choices and children's interests.**

Many practitioners feel secure in having planned in fine detail up to a term or half a term in advance, because they know what they are doing and can feel well prepared. However, keeping to such long-term plans cannot possibly be responsive to children, so if you want to prepare in advance you need to be prepared to change what you have planned according to children's interests.

For example, if you have planned to do a topic on space in the second week of term and on the Tuesday you have planned to make a planet Jupiter from papier maché, but on that day itself the children are actually interested in the postman that visited, then you may need to drop your plans and think of activities based around

Free flow play; children have moved from dressing up to the construction area

the postman. This could involve children writing letters, buying or making stamps, posting letters or making a letterbox in the setting for them to send letters and parcels to one another.

But there is a deeper question here, and that is whether planned themes can really ever be truly responsive to children's interests? Are children really interested in minibeasts every first half of the summer term?

If you take everything into consideration having topics makes planning much harder, whereas if you allow the children to guide your planning, the planning can become far more simple and straightforward and will ensure the children will be interested and motivated.

Long-term plans

A long-term plan is a loose and fluid plan incorporating your continuous provision. It is a guide for practice and helps to ensure that through your continuous provision you are providing a balance of opportunities and experiences for the children both indoors and outdoors, that also support the children's emotional development. Although long-term plans are time-consuming to complete, you only need to do them once, and review regularly.

As a staff team you need to discuss how the ethos of the setting is going to be reflected in your long-term plan and therefore in your provision. By ethos we mean your individual beliefs and passions as to the importance of early years education and your beliefs in what is best for the children in your setting.

Long-term plans can be broken down into several sub-headings, which may include the following:

- Learning opportunities – provide a list.

- Key areas of learning – whilst every area of provision provides valuable learning across all of the areas of learning and development, some spaces promote certain areas of development more.

- Resources.

- Various activities within this area – e.g. in the sandpit area you could suggest hiding treasure.

- The role of the adult in supporting learning – including vocabulary to introduce to children.

- Organisation – you may need this heading to consider how the resources are organised so that they are easily accessible to children, how they are checked for safety, how many children are allowed at an activity at any one time etc.

Often some of the areas of your provision will repeat what is written about other areas, but this is due to the holistic nature of child development and learning. It is important that all staff have access to and are involved in creating long-term plans, so that they can witness for themselves how all experiences intertwine and are reliant on another area working.

For your long-term plans to work you need a rich learning environment. The learning environment needs to be structured and well organised in order to allow teaching to happen and for children to make their own choices and decisions, and give them challenges, this will help them to learn and develop. If you get the learning environment just right then

Accessibility of resources is essential

everything else will follow, children almost cannot help but to thrive and learn in the correct surroundings across all areas of learning. The learning environment will include safety considerations so children can feel secure and safe.

As discussed long-term plans will take a good deal of time to create as for every area you need to ask what you want the child to learn from the experiences on offer and therefore what opportunities you need to offer

to develop new skills. In all activities that are planned there should be the opportunity for children to practice the skills they have acquired and develop new skills. There should be the chance to learn new concepts and begin to understand them. Children can develop a positive attitude to learning through exciting and stimulating activities and open-ended resources.

It is vital to remember that children learn across all areas of learning and not under subject headings: children learn about mathematical concepts by playing with the water e.g. seeing how many small jugs of water it takes to fill a large jug. This means that practitioners need to be aware of all the learning opportunities available within all areas of provision and activities on offer and be aware how to support each child's development.

Planning the learning environment

The setting itself will have a large impact on how you plan your environment. Every setting is different in character: from purpose-built buildings, to large day nurseries with separate rooms, to village halls and private homes for childminders. Each type of setting has benefits as well as challenges However, whatever your setting you need to plan carefully so that in the course of a session every area of learning is covered. In order to ensure that provision is exciting and varied it is recommended to have available the below resources:

- Mark making areas or graphics.

- Sand – both wet and dry sand should be offered.

- Water.

- Malleable materials – e.g. play dough.

- Maths area.

- Home corner.

- Role-play area (separate from home corner).

- Painting.

- Book corner.

- IT area.

- Construction.

- Physical area – e.g. climbing frame.

- Music.

- Woodwork area/workshop.

- Messy play.

- Exploration and investigation area.

- Small world.

- Open-ended resources.

- Games and puzzles.

Where these activities are placed within the room(s) will impact their effectiveness and your planning. On top of the established areas available for child-initiated play there will be planned adult-led activities e.g. cooking, planting. It is important to get the environment right fairly quickly because children need to come into familiar surroundings knowing that something that was there yesterday will still be there today and not moved to the opposite side of the room.

Children also need to know over time that they can access everything that you have. This may not be possible everyday because of the type of setting but if you can't have everything out consider making a book of photos of all your resources so that children can choose what they want out. Do also consult children as to what they want out. You can do this by giving children a sticker with a happy face to put on what they want out. Children who have little or no vocabulary will be able to communicate in this way.

The EPPE report says that:

'...children develop and learn better when both their interests and needs are met'.

Child and key carer looking at the self-selection book together

Short-term plans

Short-term planning involves the 'nitty gritty' planning of how your medium-term plans will be put into place, and how you will respond to individual children's learning and development needs, as identified through observations. **You must remember that children's learning should not be target driven. It is appropriate to identify what you want the child to learn in a way and make correct provision and appropriate adult support, but not to insist that the child learns something.** Many activities can cover several areas of learning but you really only want to identify one or two things that you want the child to learn from a given activity or it will become complicated and confusing for the child and also frustrating for staff.

Your short-term plans will need to be adjusted from day to day and even hour to hour to meet the needs of your children. Do not be afraid to annotate your plans and write all over them, even change them completely in response to what is happening. If an activity is simply not engaging the children, rather than plugging away at it clear it away and do something else, it doesn't matter if things go wrong.

Your short-term plans will need to show that what you provide is suitable and intended for the children who are attending, they will need to link to observations and to what you are wanting the children to learn. There also needs to be space within plans for child-initiated activities. Many practitioners complicate their short-term plans by adding in aspects of continuous provision – this doesn't need to be there because as its name suggests it's always there and has already been planned for.

Planning for individual children

You don't always need to plan separate activities for all the children in your care. One activity may meet the needs of five of them in different ways and all you have to do is write these children's initials on your planning, and link your planning to an observation to assess how this activity will meet that child's needs. Your short-term plans can be used to identify the focus for the next observation on a child.

Individual plans are plans for individual children. You may carry out individual plans because you want to look at a child more closely, perhaps because you think you may have identified an issue or a special need and want to focus on that. You may write individual plans because of a significant achievement, or your setting may write individual plans for each child as a matter of best practice.

You need to be clear on individual plans what developmental area you are working on, what stage the child is at now, and how to develop that in a relevant and appropriate way. Research has shown that children have 'critical periods' of development – that certain things always happen at a certain time and that you must not miss these critical periods. Jerome Bruner says that "having a certain kind of experience at one point in development has a profoundly different impact on future behaviours than having the same experience at any other point of development". This means that as practitioners we need to be aware of these critical periods and use them to help the children within your care.

Children also have 'sensitive periods of development' which are much the same as critical periods but they span longer periods of time. For example walking happens within a sensitive period, but a child can learn to walk over a fairly long period of time – anything from 10 months to three years. Individual plans need to encompass sensitive and critical periods. However, you must take into account that these periods are also when a child is most vulnerable and if forced by an adult to take what they are interested in and turn it into a formal lesson they are likely to become quickly disinterested and resist learning. For example, if a child is interested in dinosaurs and you decide to teach that child about the different names of all the dinosaurs, how long each one is, and what

Your short-term plans will need to be adjusted from day to day

they eat it may be too much too soon for that child and they will lose interest completely.

In your planning and provision you need to ensure you reflect a balance of child-initiated and adult-led experiences both indoors and out. This is not only a statutory requirement of the EYFS, but will also help you to ensure that you are providing broad and balanced experiences for the children.

The DCSF (2009) document *Playing, Learning and Interacting* provides clear definitions of both child-initiated and adult-led experiences to help you understand how to spot them in the setting.

> *'Child-initiated activity ... is wholly decided upon by the child, based on the child's own motivation and remains under the child's control. It may involve play of many types…'*

Remember if you had anything to do with it, it isn't child-initiated. This means you don't guide or influence the child; you let them choose from your continuous provision facilitating the free-flow play.

For children to have optimum opportunities you need to have a varied and full continuous provision. For example, there needs to be a choice of construction toys, not just stickle bricks because it is Monday and this is the activity you normally play with on Monday. Restrictions that you put on resources mean that children will not be able to develop an idea or make the most of learning possibilities. Stimulation is the key, and this can be provided through variety that promotes challenge, which is achievable.

You need to ensure that you are proving plenty of open-ended resources. An open-ended resource is one that has no specific purpose or function, but can be created into anything from the child's

imagination. If everything you provide for children has a clear purpose and function, a classic example being a shape sorter, there is risk that children will lack stimulation and the opportunity to interpret the creative and endless possibilities that more open-ended resources can have. Of course, resources with a specific purpose do have a place, but they shouldn't be the only resources on offer.

A good example of an open-ended resource is a treasure basket. Do take care to refresh and replace the items in the basket regularly, as even open-

Case study: How do you structure your planning?

Corinne Finlay, Early Years Professional, Townhill Early Years Centre, Southampton

Long-term plans

The long-term provision outlines the planned celebrations and visits diarised for the nursery throughout the academic year. In addition, our continuous provision is based on the EYFS' Themes and Characteristics of effective learning. Every area of the provision i.e. routines, outdoors, ICT, the nature area plus many more are all cross-referenced to the EYFS Themes and Characteristics of effective learning to ensure we are providing opportunities for children to develop through the Early Years Foundation Stage.

Short-term plans

EYFS Aspects Sheets: these sheets contain the Aspects for each of the broad areas of development. Each Key Person has a sheet located in their 'Big Floor Books' as a point of reference to identify what aspects have been covered, and which still need to be included.

In addition, we keep a record of individual children's next steps and targets in the Key Person's Big Floor Books, to enable the Key Person to incorporate the children's interests and next steps.

A big floor book is a reference book for key carers to track their key children's progress through the development matters of the seven areas of learning and development of the EYFS.

Observations of the children during their time at nursery are recorded on stickers, then transferred into the child's individual 'Learning Stories' book. These observations inform the children's next steps and ensure their individual needs are incorporated through everyday child-initiated activities.

We also have Individual Needs Sheets located at key areas around the play room, to ensure that all adults working in those areas are able to provide the right support for individual children's learning.

ended resources can become stale after time.

Commitment card 4.1 of the EYFS Play and Exploration states that practitioners should:

> *'Provide flexible resources that can be used in many different ways to facilitate children's play and exploration. These might include lengths of plastic guttering, tubing and watering cans near the sand and water play areas; lengths of fabric and clothes pegs in a box; large paintbrushes and buckets near the*

outside tap; boxes, clotheshorses, old blankets and tablecloths to make dens and shelters.'

When planning your continuous provision you should consider the following:

- Do all practitioners working in the setting have a clear understanding of the objectives of the provision?

- Are materials of a high standard, clean, safe and accessible and open-ended?

Case study

A nursery nurse describes planning in a nursery class of an infant school, working with children aged 3-4 years who attend either a morning or afternoon session.

We have two planned, adult-led activities everyday. These take place at the same time as the children are engaging with the continuous provision. If we have planned well the children will usually choose to come and access one or both of these activities. We select activities based on the need for skill development identified through observations, if we feel it is something the children might be interested in. Children's interests are identified through formal or informal observation, or even just an idea that we have. This all means that we can introduce new experiences to the children.

Sometimes we plan a week in advance and perhaps annotate our plans if we feel we need to change what we have planned, or sometimes we just a plan two or three days ahead and add more to our plans as the week progresses.

- Are areas visually defined using furniture, carpets, labelling or shelving?

- Is equipment stored in a variety of containers, which are easily accessible to the children and clearly labelled?

- Do children have access to all the necessary equipment so that they can be independent in following through ideas e.g. are masking tape, glue and scissors freely available?

- Do equipment and materials in each area underpin and develop literacy skills, e.g. do they provide a variety of mark making experiences, notebooks, and non-fiction books?

- Is free flow play allowed, and do children know where equipment belongs?

Your continuous provision is the basis of your learning environment and freely facilitates your child-initiated experiences. A child-initiated experience may lead into an adult-led experience, and conversely an adult-led experience may lead into a child-initiated experience. If the flow of the experiences of the setting and if your planning is effective they should compliment each other.

Adult-led experiences

So what is an adult-led experience? If we return to the DCSF (2009) document *Playing, Learning and Interacting*, it describes adult-led experiences as follows:

'Adult-led experiences are those, which adults initiate. The activities are not play and children are likely not to see them as play, but they should be playful – with activities presented to children, which are as open-ended as possible, with elements of imagination and active exploration that will increase the interest and motivation for children.'

Our adult-led experiences are planned in response to a child's interest or need that are either identified through an observation or picked up on. They may be introduced as a learning opportunity that is too good to miss or because you feel the children will benefit from experiencing something new.

The adult-led experience should be integral to the general activity session of the day and be conducted simultaneously within the continuous

Use of open-ended play materials

provision. They should not be viewed as something that everyone sits down together to do at the same time. A key carer may plan an activity for their key group, but it should also be accessible for other children.

So how do you create a balance between the child-initiated and adult-led experiences? There is no definitive target, and it is not an equal balance, but rather a balance that best meets the children's needs. Therefore, the balance should be weighted towards the child-initiated.

Remember that it is through observing and watching child-initiated experiences that you can clearly see where children are at and what they enjoy, as they are naturally showing you their knowledge and understanding.

Children are given the opportunity of choosing an activity for the session from the flip books.

The benefits of adult-led activities

- Can focus on developing a skill or an interest.

- You can extend learning in a way appropriate for the individual child.

- Helps you get to know the children.

- An ideal opportunity for a colleague to observe the children doing the activity, which can inform future planning.

- You can scaffold the child's learning.

- It can help identify learning styles and schemas.

- You can encourage the children to interact with peers who they may not normally interact with.

- Introducing a new idea or concept.

So why can't we use themes and topics, as we've always used them in the past?

Research and evidence has shown that children learn much more effectively if activities and experiences are presented to them that are meaningful and set in an appropriate context for the children. For something to have meaning for a child it must be something that they are genuinely interested in and that they find stimulating.

The EYFS encourages practitioners to be spontaneous and responsive to children, but if we know that this month's theme is transport, and the theme of the week is cars then it restricts both practitioners and children. It is restrictive in that it does not allow for flexibility or spontaneity in terms of responding to the children. How do you know in a month's time what the children are going to be interested in and where they are going to be developmentally?

Annotating or changing plans is seen as good practice as it shows that you are being responsive to the children. If your plans are too prescriptive and governed by themes and topics, the plans themselves become harder to annotate and change.

Observations are intended to enable practitioners to identify next steps for each child, but this becomes difficult to do if those next steps have to fit into next week's planned topic of houses and homes.

But, planning without themes and topics is so much harder!

Anything that involves change from old ways of working always seems hard at first. However, once you get used to a more flexible and spontaneous form of planning you will find it much easier. You are putting yourself under much less pressure in trying to plan in a flexible way, and in essence the children are doing the planning for you if you listen to them and watch what they are telling you.

Should we not plan then to explore the different seasons?

Planning is important, but should be treated in a relaxed way. Think about the centres of interest that you may want to introduce at certain times of the year that you feel will be of interest and benefit to the children, e.g. spring and autumn. Don't be fixed and rigid about these themes, just introduce a few ideas about that particular season and observe what the children respond to and how. This will enable you to decide how long to explore autumn and where to go next.

I don't feel safe not having a topic to structure children's work around. How do I know what to do and how can I assess what children have learnt?

You are bound to feel uncertain at first, but through the use of observations and careful adult interactions with children you will still find plenty of exciting things to do, and you will be able to record children's learning in an even more detailed way than before because it will be relevant to them as an individual.

What do children need to know and/or understand before they can...?

Hold a paintbrush

Children need to have had plenty of opportunity to develop and build their fine motor and manipulative skills, through building muscle strength and development. The muscles that control the fingers come from the forearm. So lots of messy play and play dough is essential to develop these skills and build muscles. Children then gradually gain control and the pincer grip develops so they can hold a paintbrush. Children will need to start with larger objects such as a sponges, as the smaller the hand the larger the object needs to be that the hand can hold. Children also need to have explored paint using their hands to understand its properties, what it feels like and how it behaves.

Put on their shoes

They need to have the balance and coordination to sit, bend down and hold onto their shoe. They also need to have the strength to push their foot into the shoe and the patience to persevere with this skill.

Make a Chinese lantern for Chinese New Year

An understanding of the purpose of making a Chinese lantern and what Chinese New Year is about. Children need to have had plenty of opportunity to develop the skills necessary, e.g. fine motor skills, using scissors, hand and eye coordination, and understand the property of glue and paint. Children should be able to make the lantern for themselves without following an adult's model.

Sit in a group for circle time

Remember circle time is not about who is here today, or the weather, or show and tell, but rather about a focused discussion about a specific subject where children may be invited to contribute, perhaps by holding a teddy when it is their turn to speak. You may use props to support the discussion. To do this children need to be able to sit and concentrate for a period of time, perhaps 10 minutes, they need to have the language to articulate and contribute to the discussion and the confidence to be involved.

Write their own name

Before children can write their own names they need to have practised many gross motor skills, as well as fine motor skills. They also need to be able to co-ordinate both hands. Children will need to have had plenty of mark making experiences using their fingers and some tools, remembering that the smaller the hand the larger the object needs to be. Only when these skills have been refined will a child be able to hold a pencil in order to begin to write. Children need to have already seen their names written down and have seen their name being written. Simply writing on top of an adult's prescribed writing model will not help the child to develop the necessary muscle development and skills, nor will holding the child's hand and guiding it to write. Remember that the child's given name will have an influence on their success at writing it, e.g. 'Michael' is a lot more difficult to write and to spell than the name 'Anna'.

Ask a question

The language and understanding to be able to pose a question, to understand why a question is needed, and the ability to remember to wait to listen for the answer.

How a child-initiated experience could lead to an adult-led activity or experience

Child-initiated	Adult-led
A child absorbed in messy play with jelly cubes and ice cubes	Freeze a balloon filled with water, once frozen take the balloon off the ice. Put the frozen balloon out with torches for the children to shine on the ice and magnifying glasses and encourage the children to explore the balloon. What does it feel like? What can they see through the magnifying glasses?
Children burying treasure in the digging area outside	Bury some objects for the children to find. Have a selection of collecting pots with a number on the lid or a picture or pictures of objects in the setting, encourage the children to find objects corresponding with what is on the lid of their pot.
Using the digital camera	Take a series of photos around the setting at a funny angle and see if the children can match the place in the setting to the photo.
Drinks factory in the water tray	Offer a selection of fruit juices and water, both sparkling and still so the children can select and make their own fruit juice cocktails. Alternatively you could use milk and fruit to make milkshakes or smoothies.
Children are role playing holding a picnic, they move their picnic things from the home corner to the outdoor area	Make sandwiches and have a picnic during story time whilst reading *The Giant Jam Sandwich*.
Children are splashing in the puddles outdoors	Create lots of small puddles outside on a sunny day; encourage the children to draw round them with chalk to see the evaporation.

Continuous Provision Long Term Plan

Area:	
Resources:	
Personal, Social and Emotional Development:	**Communication and Language:**
Physical Development:	**Literacy:**
Mathematics:	**Understanding the World:**
Expressive Arts and Design:	**Characteristics of Effective Learning:**
Possible enhancement:	

Weekly planning sheet

Week beginning: 17 May 2010	Additions and changes to the continuous provision to support child-initiated experiences	Adult-led experiences and activities	Links to the EYFS	Notes and evaluation
Monday	**INDOOR** Add real kitchen utensils to the home corner. **Links to observations:** B obs 1	**INDOOR** Play with cornflour and use the dictaphone. **Links to observations:** A obs 1, E obs 1	EAD, exploring and using the meadia and materials 8-26mths	The dictaphone kept jamming and the batteries ran out quickly, but the children had fun helping to work out how to make it work.
	OUTDOOR Make hard hats, fluorescent jackets and clipboards available outside. **Links to observations:**	**OUTDOOR** **Links to observations:**	UW, Technology, 30-50mths	
Tuesday	**INDOOR** **Links to observations:**	**INDOOR** Making fairy cakes. **Links to observations:** B obs 1	UW, World, 30-50mths	
	OUTDOOR **Links to observations:**	**OUTDOOR** **Links to observations:**		
Wednesday	**INDOOR** **Links to observations:**	**INDOOR** **Links to observations:**		
	OUTDOOR **Links to observations:**	**OUTDOOR** **Links to observations:**		Extension activity, using wallpaper outside for hand and foot printing.
Thursday	**INDOOR** **Links to observations:**	**INDOOR** **Links to observations:**		
	OUTDOOR **Links to observations:**	**OUTDOOR** **Links to observations:**		
Friday	**INDOOR** **Links to observations:**	**INDOOR** **Links to observations:**		
	OUTDOOR **Links to observations:**	**OUTDOOR** **Links to observations:**		

Please note that a completed planning sheet in a setting would be much fuller than the above example. Remember that not every experience will link to an observation, particularly if you are introducing a new experience or consolidating experiences.

*if an activity is not linked to an observation, it should reflect the children's interest or be planned for skill development or something new you wish to introduce

	MONDAY	TUESDAY	WEDNESDAY	THURSDAY	FRIDAY
Planned Adult-Led Experience					
Link to observations*					
Links to EYFS					
Next step/evaluation					
Planned Adult-Led Experience					
Link to observations*					
Links to EYFS					
Next step/evaluation					
Additions to the continuous provision					
Key interests noted during session/day					
Characteristics of effective learning seen in practice					

Weekly planner

Week beginning				
Key interests and points from observations week ending (previous week):				
Additions and changes to the continuous provision to support child-initiated experiences	Links to EYFS	Adult-led experiences and activities	Links to EYFS	Notes and evaluation	Next steps

The planning cycle

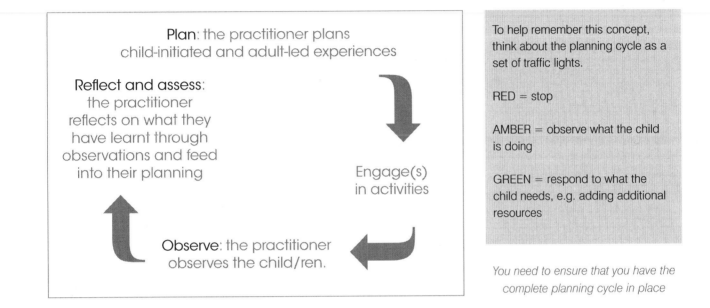

Plan: the practitioner plans child-initiated and adult-led experiences

Reflect and assess: the practitioner reflects on what they have learnt through observations and feed into their planning

Engage(s) in activities

Observe: the practitioner observes the child/ren.

To help remember this concept, think about the planning cycle as a set of traffic lights.

RED = stop

AMBER = observe what the child is doing

GREEN = respond to what the child needs, e.g. adding additional resources

You need to ensure that you have the complete planning cycle in place

The planning cycle is the process used to describe the link between observations and planning. You need to ensure that you have the complete cycle in place; otherwise you are not completing the statutory requirements of the EYFS. The planning cycle is the format which has been used in early years for many years and is not new.

Many settings have a form of the planning cycle in place but not a complete cycle; it is as if their cycle has a puncture.

The planning cycle in practice

So how does the planning cycle relate to practice? It can be seen in a variety of different ways.

A practitioner notices a child engaging with a particular activity or experience and realises that their experience can be enhanced with the addition of a particular resource or resources. The practitioner adds the resource and annotates the planning sheet with information on what happened.

Alternatively, it may be that what a practitioner has seen the child do guides the practitioner as to the choice of story for story time. This method of implementing the planning cycle informally is just as important as a more formal approach. The informal approach shows that the practitioner fully understands the importance of responding to children and being spontaneous in their approach. It also demonstrates that they have a clear understanding of the concept that annotating plans to show spontaneity is good practice. This is a good starting point for a less confident or inexperienced practitioner, as there is limited paperwork involved.

If you are a team leader encourage practitioners to get used to the idea of responding spontaneously to the children, using this informal moment-by-moment approach to the planning cycle before encouraging them to use a more formal approach.

A more formal approach to the planning cycle is to take your lead from the planned learning environment.

1. The child engages with the environment.

2. The practitioner observes the child, and records what they see the child do.

3. The practitioner reflects on the observation and identifies what they have learnt about the child and the appropriate next steps are for the child indicating these clearly on the observation sheet.

4. New plans clearly show what new steps are recommended for individual children.

Remember, as has been mentioned in previous chapters, these next steps could be additions to the learning environment, adaptations to the routine, or planned adult-led experiences, whatever is best for the child.

It is this noting of next steps and the follow-through on planning that is crucial to completing the planning cycle, and it is this very aspect, which proves to be a stumbling block for many settings. Adopting the informal and formal approach though certainly aids understanding and helps to ensure that this cycle becomes embedded in practice.

Clear understanding of and awareness of the importance of the planning cycle can support practitioners to implement systems and processes effectively. This does not mean that you have to observe what you plan to do in response to what the child has done from a previous observation, as this would mean that you were narrowing the field of potential development opportunities for the child. You just need to complete the cycle.

In the DCSF document *Learning, Playing and Interacting: Good Practice in the Early Years Foundation Stage* (2009) the benefits of the planning and observation process for children are described as follows:

> '[M]eeting children where they are, showing them the next open door, and helping them to walk through it. It means being a partner with children, enjoying with them the *power of curiosity and the thrill of finding out what they can do.'*

The practice of the planning cycle stems from many of Vygotsky's ideas in his theory of the zone proximal development. In simple terms, Vygotsky believed that every child is at a natural level of learning and development, but with support from educators or more experienced peers children have the potential to achieve beyond that level. By observing children and responding through your plans to what children need and their interests your practice is building on Vygostky's theories, you are following through the theory of Vygotsky, be it through child-initiated or adult-led experiences.

That explains the connection to short-term planning; the planning cycle also supports effective individual forward

Case study

Kim Goldhagen, Pre-School Leader, Cheddington Pre-School

Children's individual needs are raised as a regular agenda item at our fortnightly staff meetings. This gives key carers an opportunity to share their observations and knowledge of specific children to ensure that their individual needs are being met.

Case study

A day nursery manager says that in her nursery they ask the parents to make notes on the observations and they also make notes of information from the parents about what the children have done, e.g. stayed the night at their Grandma's.

Case study

Corinne Finlay, Early Years Professional, Town Hill Early Years Centre, Southampton

"We involve parents by inviting them to parents evenings and inviting them to contribute to observations. The setting also has a monthly newsletter advising parents what each key group has been doing."

Key carer relationship

The starting point of planning for the key person will be the information supplied by the child's parents or guardians

planning, as part of your summative assessment, which is explained in the next chapter. The key difference with short-term is you are reflecting on and assessing a single observation or occurrence, whereas with summative assessment you are looking at a collection of observations to help you forward plan.

Involving all staff in the observation and planning process is essential, as this ensures that:

■ The needs of all children in the setting are met.

■ There is a consistency and continuity in approach from all staff, with no gaps in the planning and observation cycle.

■ There is a common understanding of the aims and objectives of the observation and planning system.

■ The process will be effective.

Practitioners' ability to be able to plan and observe is a crucial part of their role within the setting, in stimulating and supporting the child to reach beyond their current stage, both through the formal and informal cycles.

The key person

The key person has a critical role to play in the planning cycle. As part of good practice and as an essential part of their role, **the key person needs to have a clear understanding and awareness of where all their key children are in terms of their development, be aware of any specific individual needs and their likes and dislikes.**

The starting point of planning for the key person will be the information supplied by the child's parents when the child first begins in the setting.

This is then built upon with initial observations carried out during the settling in process. Hopefully this involvement of the child's parents/carers will continue.

The key person then uses this knowledge and information to support the planning process. On commitment card 1.1 Child Development of the Early Years Foundation Stage pack, it states under reflecting in practice:

Think about each child in the group. Consider their:

■ Unique development.

■ Individual interests.

■ Communication style.

■ Learning style.

This is a good exercise to do every so often so that the key person can gauge if there are any gaps in their knowledge of the child and help to identify if they are using their knowledge of the child effectively.

The key person's role does not have to be about planning on an individual basis but, should reflect the needs of the individual in planning for the group. Several children may have slightly different needs, but they might all be met through the same activity or experience. The ability to be able to identify this and follow through is about time and experience. The key person needs to feel supported in this role by their leader in a group setting, or development worker or network co-ordinator if working in a home-based setting. There should be regular opportunity for practitioners to discuss their key children with colleagues.

Key carers also need to have a good understanding and awareness of child development, the ways in which children learn, observations and the planning cycle.

The key person needs to continue involving parents, encouraging them to share observations of their child at home. This doesn't mean that the parent should formally record observations of their child, but rather the key person should ask the parent to share their observations verbally. Parental observations should be valued and kept in the child's profile. The key carer needs to share with the parent what they are supporting the child to work towards next in terms of their development, and share their observations with the parents and invite comment. The daily diary used by childminders or daily sheets used by day nurseries are ways of inviting comment from parents about their child.

Children themselves also need to be involved in the planning process. This can be achieved in a number of ways:

- Ask the children what their interests are and you may put up a chart or pictorial representation to show this and to indicate that you will be including their interest in the learning environment.

- Ask children to take photos of what they like in the setting.

- Ask children to put smiley face stickers on what they like and enjoy doing, and unsmiley faces and stickers on what they don't enjoy.

- Use photos of the resources for the children to look at and then indicate what they enjoy and like.

You should then note on your plans where you have responded to this feedback from children in order to complete that aspect of the planning cycle.

Ask children what their interests are and put up pictures to show this

Case study

Mary Jefferson Cobb, Childminder, Buckinghamshire

"I observe individual children during open-ended play times. Taking into account each child's developmental stages, I can balance the child/adult experience. Written observations, individual plans plus weekly/daily planning, all contribute to my assessment of each child's individual needs and enable me to plan the next steps. Observations provide me with a wealth of information on each child, and this is the basis of my future planning and ongoing observations.

I show the links between my observations and planning through the 'Next Step' box on my observation sheets, in which I make notes for future planning. Then on my planning sheet I have an 'Additional Notes & Links to Observations' box where I make notes for future observations, as well as indicating links from previous observations.

I involve parents by taking time to chat to them at drop off and collection times, during which we swap observations of their child. A daily diary is used for each child which is given to parents, and in which I write a mini observation or day of the child. Once per term, each child's portfolio of observations, is taken home by the parents for them to digest and return, with comments if they wish."

All about assessment

The Early Years Foundation Stage and the Ofsted inspection framework put a clear emphasis on the importance of assessment and using that to show children's progress, taking into account starting points and using observation to support these assessments, this includes the progress check at two.

People often shy away from assessment, usually because of a lack of understanding of what it involves. Assessment however is an essential part of the observation process, and without assessment you cannot fully utilise the information you have gleaned from observations. It is certainly not about testing.

In the Statutory Framework it states that:

'Assessment okays an important part in helping parents, carers and practitioners to recognise children's progress, understand their needs and to plan activities and support.'

Assessment is about tracking children's progress so you know that they are moving forward. This tracking needs to reflect all seven areas of learning and development.

There are two key processes in assessment: formative and summative assessment. The formative assessment provides the evidence for the summative assessment. In the DCSF document *Progress Matters: Reviewing and Enhancing Young Children's Development* (2009) the process of assessment is described as:

- **Gathering** – information on children's learning and development.

- **Using** – information to support children's learning and development.

- **Summarising** – information to track children's progress.

- **Using summary information** – to support children's progress.

The first two items describe formative assessment and the last two summative assessments.

Formative assessment

Formative assessment is about the process of observing children over a period of time and collecting evidence, the evidence being your observations. You may also add to this evidence photographs and samples of the children's work e.g. paintings and mark making.

Through the collection of observations and other evidence you have on a particular child you can build up the story of their individual journey of development and learning. It's a story that continually changes and evolves with each little twist and turn, never end, and you can never be exactly sure what is going to happen next.

Formative assessment is about observing children over a period of time

Summative assessment is about looking at your formative assessments gathered over a period of time, perhaps six weeks or a term and reflecting on those assessments and identifying what it tells you about the child in terms of where that child is developmentally and where they need to go next.

Summative assessment

This process of summative assessment allows you to see how a child has progressed and moved on. If there is a particular area of learning and development where they are moving at a faster pace or an area where perhaps they appear to have stagnated in their developmental journey. You can also see if they are any gaps in your observations. You make the decision about the child's progress using the 'Development Matters' document of the Early Years Foundation Stage (2012).

Just as you would with your observations, you need to conduct summative assessments objectively and from a position of enquiry, actively seeking to make discoveries about the child. The accuracy and validity of the summative assessment is very much dependent on the quality and variety of observations made about each child. The broader the picture that has been built up of the child the more effective the assessment will be in helping to determine where the child needs to go next.

So what does good quality assessment require?

- Incorporates the three prime areas of learning and development for all children and the specific areas of learning and development where applicable.

- Include observations of both child-initiated and adult-led experiences.

- Emphasis on what children can do and what they can nearly do.

- A range and variety of observations to work with.

- Time to reflect and draw conclusions.

- You need evidence of the process and not just the product: it is in the

You need to conduct a summative assessment objectively and from a position of enquiry

doing or the playing that the learning and development takes place.

- Practitioners with a clear understanding of the aims and objectives of the process and of the seven areas of learning and development.

Summative assessments may be logged using an assessment sheet or an individual plan, which incorporate the seven areas of learning and development individually. The information can guide you in terms of where the child needs to go next and the support they may need. This can be shared with parents and possible activities to carry out at home can be identified.

As part of this process, you need to ask yourselves about the individual child and discuss with colleagues how information gathered about individual children correlates with others and

can then be used to support learning and development within the group.

You need to think about:

- What the implications are of your observations?

- How to extend language opportunities for the child?

- How can you support the child's ability to foster relationships?

- How can you review and plan the learning environment as a response to findings?

- How can you respond to what has been observed and extend learning and development in all seven areas and does one area need more support or attention than another?

So what is the best method of recording your summative assessment? As with all observation and planning paperwork in the early years, it is the choice of the individual setting. The decision of how to proceed needs to be made whilst thinking about what best gives you the necessary information and a clear overview of each child.

On the accompanying CD-Rom, we have provided two examples of a summative assessment sheet, one for children under two and for children over two. Both can be used in order to reflect on your observations and assess where the child is at in terms of progress in the relevant areas of learning and development.

Assessment supports the focus on the thoughts and knowledge of the child and helps you to act spontaneously with the child, knowing when an appropriate learning opportunity has arisen. It also helps you to see if the child is moving forward and if so, what you are providing for them is stimulating and effective.

The assessment process also provides a chance for you to reflect on the implications of your own practice on the child's progress, thinking about how you can best support the child. It can be useful to consider your practice in the following way:

- **STOP – is there something in your practice you need to stop doing?**

- **START – is there something new you would like to implement in your practice?**

- **CARRY ON – is there something that you are pleased with and doing really well that you want to continue?**

It is this tracking of progress, perhaps kept as a learning journey that not only enables you to see how a child has progressed in that particular assessment period, but also over longer periods of time, e.g. their time at that particular setting.

From this assessment, you should be able to identify the following:

- The needs of the child in terms of planning the environment and specific experiences.

- Identify what they can do, can nearly do and what they need to be able to do to develop further.

- Provide information about their level of play, development, interest and interactions with others.

- Help practitioners to identify their own effectiveness in terms of the provision and their support of the child.

- Any areas that need specific focus.

You can use this tracking of progress to help refresh your memories at the beginning of a term, or after a child returns from a holiday or prolonged period of absence. You must remember though that these absences from the setting will impact on where the child is at on their return.

Assessment can also be used to inform other practitioners, particularly when a child in a day nursery moves rooms and has a new key person or to support transitions outside the setting.

Why no checklists?

A checklist is about trying to categorise children into specific boxes and not thinking holistically about the individual child. It is very tempting to tick off something inaccurately, without recognising that children won't do everything. They develop at their own rates and in their own ways and a summative assessment reflects individuality. A summative assessment doesn't put the child under pressure of a 'test' as it reflects your observations and knowledge of the child.

THE PROGRESS CHECK AT TWO

AIM OF THE CHECK

- It is a statutory requirement

- Part of the early intervention initiative

- To identify where the child is at in all of the three prime areas and if necessary identify any problems in the three prime areas, and working early on to support them

- Encouraging dialogue and communication between the setting and the child's parents

- Supporting good practice in relation to summative assessments to monitor children's progress.

WHEN TO DO THE CHECK

- Between the ages of 24-36 months, but as near to 24 months as possible, so parents can share it with their health visitor at the 2-year-old health and development check if they wish

- The check needs to be carried out by the child's key carer and shared with the parents at a convenient time

- Remember to ensure the child is settled and hasn't experienced any recent emotional upheaval e.g. birth of a new sibling which may have affected their development

- If a child joins your setting between the ages of 24-36 months and has previously not attended an early years setting, once they have settled in you need to carry out the check

- If the child attends two settings, the setting where they spend the most time is responsible for carrying out the check, but it is good practice to exchange information.

HOW TO DO

- The check is based on your ongoing observations and knowledge of the child in the three prime areas

- A summary needs to be written on where the child is at either in general on each area or individually on each aspect of each area

- You must note in each aspect of each area which development phase the child is at

- You may wish to include information about the child and the characteristics of effective learning and their key interests

- Include on the form how long the child has attended the setting and how many sessions they attend a week, as this is significant in terms of how well you may know the child

- Identify any significant next steps for the child

- If the child is not progressing in any of the three prime areas, you need to state how you are going to support them.

INCLUDING PARENTS

- The purpose of the check and why it is being carried out and that it is based on what you have observed and your knowledge of the child

- That you will share it with them at a mutually convenient time and that they will be able to comment on the check about what they have noticed about their child's development

- The development phases, so they are aware of the individual nature of development and that the phases overlap because they are not fixed boundaries but suggest a typical range of development

- The prime areas and their aspects

- What will happen if their child is not progressing

- Explain that they can then share the check with their health visitor

- Tell them they keep the check and you will put a copy in their child's profile that you keep, to help you monitor their progress.

Monitoring and reviewing your planning, observation and assessment processes

You can pick up a lot visually, without always taking notes

Monitoring observation, assessment and planning

Managers in settings have to monitor observations and assessment carried out by practitioners ensuring they are completed accurately and to evaluate quality and consistency throughout the setting regarding the standard of observations and assessment. This includes looking at the children's learning journeys, tracking through any next steps that are identified. Planning also needs to be monitored, ensuring the appropriateness of what has been planned regarding developmental stage and how this reflects the children's needs and interests.

Cohort analysis

A cohort progress tracker and analysis should be completed at least once a year. This enables managers to look at progress children are making in all areas with an overview perspective. Comparisons should be made of progress in all areas; is there an area where, in general, children make more or less progress? Additional comparisons should be made between: boys' and girls' progress, the progress of children with English as an additional language compared to as a first language and between children with additional needs compared to no additional needs. This tracker, when completed will show any differences in the progress any of these groups are making in any areas or if overall there is a particular area of learning and development where children are making greater or lesser progress. This might indicate gaps in your provision or it might highlight gaps in practitioner knowledge relating to assessment.

Once the cohort progress tracker has been completed, an evaluation of the analysis should be completed. This should highlight any necessary action and be fed into the setting's development plan and SEF.

Reviewing

The review itself needs two stages: one where the leader in the setting analyses the effectiveness of staff in carrying out the observation and planning process, and the second involving all staff working in the setting and focusing on practicalities and understanding. As all staff are involved in observation and planning, they should all be involved in any review.

Leaders need to reflect on the following:

- Do practitioners have sufficient and appropriate skills to carry out effective observations and complete planning?

- Are all practitioners aware of the aims and objectives of the observation and planning process?

It is important that everyone is involved and on board with peer observation

- Do practitioners have realistic and appropriate expectations of the children?

- Are children making progress, including those who may be falling behind their age/stage of development expectations, and those who may be beyond their age/stage of development expectations?

- Is the learning environment supporting learning? Does it provide challenge and stimulation?

- Is an appropriate balance of child-initiated and adult-led experiences being provided both indoors and out?

- Are all seven areas of learning and development effectively provided for through the learning environment and planned activities and experiences?

- Are practitioners completing observations and planning sheets

accurately, appropriately and regularly? Is the information relevant and does it focus on the child, are observations objective?

- Are practitioners linking observations and planning to complete the planning cycle?

- Are practitioners responding to children's individual needs and interests?

The responses to these questions will give some indication as to how well the systems and processes are working and if there are any areas that need addressing. Perhaps some practitioners need up-skilling and would benefit from attending training, maybe more systematic reviews of the actual learning environment need to be carried out, perhaps some routines need
to adapted and changed.

The second stage of the review process needs to involve the whole

Cohort Progress Tracker – Prime Areas

Date completed	Personal, Social and Emotional Development												Communication and Language												Physical Development								
	Making relationships				Self confidence and self awareness				Managing feelings and behaviour				Listening and attention				Understanding				Speaking				Moving and handling				Health and self care			
	B	G	EAL	SEN	B	G	EAL	SEN	B	G	EAL	SEN	B	G	EAL	SEN	B	G	EAL	SEN	B	G	EAL	SEN	B	G	EAL	SEN	B	G	EAL	SEN
0-11 MONTHS																																
Entering																																
Developing																																
Secure																																
8-20 MONTHS																																
Entering																																
Developing																																
Secure																																
16-26 MONTHS																																
Entering																																
Developing																																
Secure																																
22-36 MONTHS																																
Entering																																
Developing																																
Secure																																
30-50 MONTHS																																
Entering																																
Developing																																
Secure																																
40-60+ MONTHS																																
Entering																																
Developing																																
Secure																																

B – boys G – girls EAL – English as an additional language SEN – Special Educational Needs

Date completed	Literacy		Mathematics		Understanding the World			Expressive Arts and Design	
	Reading	Writing	Numbers	Shape, space and measure	People and communities	The World	Technology	Exploring and using media and materials	Being imaginative
	B G EAL SEN	B G EAL SEN	B G EAL SEN	B G EAL SEN	B G EAL SEN	B G EAL SEN	B G EAL SEN	B G EAL SEN	B G EAL SEN
0-11 MONTHS Entering									
Developing									
Secure									
8-20 MONTHS Entering									
Developing									
Secure									
16-26 MONTHS Entering									
Developing									
Secure									
22-36 MONTHS Entering									
Developing									
Secure									
30-50 MONTHS Entering									
Developing									
Secure									
40-60+ MONTHS Entering									
Developing									
Secure									

Details of areas and/or aspects where there are differences in the progress children are making:

Details of areas and/or aspects where generally children are making more or less progress:

Conclusions:

Action necessary as a result of analysis:

Completed by:

Date:

staff team and gives them an opportunity to express how they feel about the process. Depending on the staff team the following reflective questions might be posed during a staff meeting facilitating this review.

- Do they understand why they are observing and planning?

- Do they have time to observe and plan and do they work together to support each other observing and planning?

- Do you have time to discuss observations in detail?

- How easy and effective do they find the methods of recording observations and planning sheets are in practice?

- Is there any way they feel the process of recording observations and planning could be streamlined?

- Do they feel confident with observing and planning?

- How do they involve parents in the planning and observation process?

It is essential that all staff are involved in this process as they will feel engaged as their opinions are being sought and valued, and also have a sense of ownership over the process. This can also help dispel any negativity towards the process. It is important that leaders and managers remember that often this negativity can derive from a lack of understanding of the process. For this process to work there needs to be support for practitioners, so that they don't feel as if they are on their own.

Once any necessary changes or alterations have been identified through this review, a process of implementation needs to be agreed and understood by all those concerned, to include a timescale and an identified review date for these changes.

Observation and planning – don't make these mistakes:

- The aim for a planned focused observation is too vague and not specific enough to guide the observation.

- Don't over plan: too much planning restricts spontaneity.

- The observation itself is not detailed enough and vague. It may describe what a child is doing in loose terms instead of providing the finer detail, e.g. "she picks up the beaker" instead of "she picks up beaker in her left hand using a grasp movement".

- Not being objective in the observation and putting in subjective opinions about what a child might be feeling.

- Not describing facial expressions or reactions, but simply saying the child is happy or excited.

- Beginning the observation by describing the surroundings or lead up to the observation, instead of just launching into the observation.

- Not showing on planning sheets how an idea links directly to an observation.

- Not identifying clear next steps on an observation, but just putting a vague idea e.g. saying a music activity, instead of stating exactly what activity.

- Not referring back to the aim when evaluating a focussed observation.

- Using checklists with no supporting observations.

- Planning too far in advance and not allowing for spontaneity and flexibility.

- Make presumptions that aren't written in the observation.

Reviewing your planning and observation procedures is, ultimately, beneficial

- Referring to skills in the evaluation that aren't evident from the observation. For example, saying the child uses scissors well when the observation makes no mention of the child using scissors.

- Not observing for long enough to get enough valuable information.

- Thinking the child is 'not doing anything' – children are always doing something, just record what you see even if they appear inactive.

- Make sure you refer to the observation in planning with the child's initials and either the date or the number of the observation.

- Remember the links to the EYFS identified on an observation relating to the actual observation do not also have to link to the area of learning of the identified next steps e.g. your links identified to the observation might be CL but the next step might link to UW.

Below are some common barriers to effective planning and observation, along with some possible solutions.

When am I supposed to find time to plan and observe?

There is a no straightforward solution to this plea! You have to provide evidence of planning and observation, as it is a statutory requirement. But quite apart from that remember you are doing it for the children to improve their experience and opportunities and bring about better outcomes. In a group setting you need to work as a team to support each other, knowing when someone is doing a focussed observation so this can be allowed for and supported within the group. Look to develop strategies to make your planning as simple and as straightforward as possible, so it becomes less time consuming, use some of the examples in this book! It is not about having folders and folders full of paperwork, but ensuring your system is effective in demonstrating how you link observations and planning together, and ensuring what is written is reflected in what is seen in the setting.

I can't provide continuous provision: we are a 'put it out and pack it away' setting in a village hall.

Yes you can; think about how you can, not simply that it is impossible. Think about storage that is easily moveable and easy to store: vegetable racks work really well and don't take up too much space. Also strong solid folding units work well and provide division for quiet areas within the hall. Have a team approach and system to putting out and packing away again, so it doesn't feel like such an onerous task. If space is limited in the hall use photos that children can use to indicate resource choices. Remember that children need to know that they can ask for equipment to be got out, just because you know you'll get it out for them do not presume that they will know that too, you need to instruct your children in how this works.

I can't provide continuous provision, I'm a childminder.

Obviously it can be extremely difficult to provide continuous provision in a home-based setting. Remember though that some choice is better than no choice. Many childminders use photographs of their resources so the children can use this as a trigger to indicate a choice. Sometimes children will need to see a toy being played with previously before they will point to it on a photograph, so make sure that you rotate what you do get out.

If we allow for free flow play the children just make a mess.

The question is how do you define a mess? This very much boils down to supervision and how we support children to know and understand where resources are kept and the importance of putting things away once they have been finished with. It is not about simply tipping things out, children need to be taught how to put things out and how to put them away. Do you use careful labelling and silhouettes to help children know where resources are kept? What strategies do you use to encourage children to help at tidy up time?

We can't have free flow between the inside and the outside because of maintaining staff to children ratios.

If you have a door directly linking your indoor and outdoor environments, there is an expectation that you will facilitate free flow between the indoors

In a group setting you need to work as a team

and outdoors. You need to look carefully at your numbers and ratios and work out the best way to facilitate this. Many settings use a band system that children put on and off as they go outside to limit numbers outside, keep choice and maintain ratios.

How do we encourage parents to contribute to the children's observations?

Include on summative assessment sheets a 'parent comment box'. You could send a card home half term, termly or three-monthly asking parents to reflect on what has happened in that term or three month period, that their child has enjoyed and anything noticed about their development.

How can I plan individually for the whole group, it's impossible!

Don't tie yourself up in knots with the planning, remember one planned activity or experience can meet the individual needs of several children in completely different ways. A finger

painting activity may support one child's manipulative skills, another child's emotional needs and another child's exploration of the medium of paint. Children will also access an activity at their own level and find ways to meet their own needs.

My planning is very complicated, with so many different pieces of paper.

If you find when someone comes in to look at your planning that it takes you 30 minutes to explain it and they are looking blank and completely dazed at the end of the explanation then it may be that you need to rethink and make it clearer and more straightforward. Don't be afraid to realise that your planning isn't working well and to scrap what you are doing and start afresh. Most problems occur by tweaking what is already happening because it becomes confusing and complicated for staff. Sadly, many practitioners have over the years been led to believe that planning means lots of paperwork rather than creating opportunities for children to learn. A setting that received support for planning said to me "It's so simple now, are you sure it's right?" It was such a relief for them – it doesn't need to be complicated, that has never been the purpose of the EYFS. All that you need to be able to do is link your planning to your observations on individual children. This doesn't mean that you have to write tons of information on the plans about how they are meeting the needs of individual children, instead simply refer the plans to the observation that identifies those needs.

My plans are always changing.

The thing is your plans should be always changing, this is good – what you need to do is write on your plans what has

One planned activity can meet the individual needs of several children

happened instead of what you planned to happen. For example, you may have planned to spend some time reading a story but it was snowing so you took advantage of that and played in the snow looking at the snowflakes and building snowmen. In this case you would cross out the story activity and write in what you did in the snow – not forgetting to include any photos you have taken in the snow if possible. It is ok that this happened, it is not a failure in anyway as it demonstrates that you have responded to children's interests and the circumstances. At other times you may need to adjust plans because something has gone wrong, but as long as you can think on your feet and make accommodation for whatever has happened this is fine.

How do I decide 'what's next'?

This is a problem for many practitioners, as it requires a good knowledge of child development and knowledge of individual children. It does get better with practice but sometimes you have to think outside the box and be creative.

My leader does all the planning and only tells me what is going to happen.

This is an issue that needs to be addressed. Key people should be involved in planning because they have carried out the observations and know the children best so they need to be involved in the next step of planning. You may be able to start by suggesting that you plan one or two activities for your key children and develop it from there. Or bring the issue up at a staff meeting explaining your need to be helping with planning. This is also about teamwork – good teamwork is essential in providing a stimulating learning environment. If you have an inspection all staff will need to be able to talk through the planning with the inspector and be aware of what they are doing for each child and why. Clearly to be able to do this all staff need to be involved in creating the plans.

Key people should be involved in planning because they know the children best

on the fact that you don't plan for Ofsted's benefit, but for the benefit of the children and the setting. It is also important to remember that Ofsted or agents acting on their behalf are acting on behalf of the government to ensure we fulfil the statutory requirements.

I don't have time to do observations, with everything else that is going on.

Part of any early years worker's job is to carry out observations and time has to be made for these. This may involve devising a rota system so that they get done.

I am worried that my spelling and grammar are poor, so I don't want other people to see them.

If you are worried about your spelling it is good to use a dictionary when writing out your observations or use spell check on the computer. It is also good to use the computer if your handwriting is illegible.

The children I have are too young to be involved in planning and observations.

It is surprising how much very young children can contribute to planning and observations. If during observations you make careful note of their body language and what it indicates, this alone will indicate what their likes and dislikes are.

I don't really understand what the observations are telling me about a child, and so I don't know what the next steps would be.

It is sometimes difficult to interpret what an observation is telling you. What have you learnt about a specific child through the observation? Sometimes it is difficult to put into words what you have learnt.

This does get better with practice and guidance; perhaps you could ask

We plan two years in advance because most children are with us for two years. We work on the same topics in a two-year cycle. We get out the crafts and see what we made two years ago, but staff are involved in planning because they choose which of the activities they want to lead and they can change them a bit if they want to.

This really has happened and is probably more widespread than we would like to admit. The problem with planning like this is that it doesn't meet the needs of the children at the setting at the time or respond to their interests. Who is to say that every cohort of children will be interested in minibeasts in the first half of the summer term of the second

year? This particular group may be interested in superheroes or princesses. The craft activities may be differentiated but they are not individual if it is more a 'here's one I made earlier' scenario. When activities have been planned far in advance children cannot be active in their learning and practitioners cannot possibly predict so far in advance what a child will learn. Children may not want to make Incy Wincy Spider, they may want to make Spiderman instead. The needs of children aside, it is very boring and unfulfilling for staff to repeat the same ideas year after year, and clearly doesn't meet the statutory requirement of tailoring plans to meet individual needs.

I do all this planning and, except for when we have an inspection, no-one else ever looks at it.

To overcome the resentment of having to do so much planning and no-one looking at it you need to stay focused a senior practitioner to mentor you through this until you feel confident. It is always beneficial to attend courses that can help your professional development and also to share ideas with others.

If I give children free reign in creative activities how can I be sure that they have learnt? For example, if they are making spiders and put ten legs on instead of eight, what have they learnt?

This is about knowing the difference between a creative activity and one that is a learning activity. It is ok to have an adult-led activity making spiders with eight legs, providing that you don't consider that to be creative, as it isn't using the child's own imagination.

There needs to be a balance of child-initiated and adult-led activities within your planning to allow children's independence, but also to support and scaffold their learning and development.

How can I involve a parent/carer who doesn't speak English?

If information can be emailed, the parents can then use a translation programme (this would be more reliable than you using one). If you have a member of staff who speaks their first language, they can share with the parent and sometimes other parents are happy to help.

How can I plan and observe a child who only attends a couple of mornings a week?

Regardless of how frequently a child attends the setting, you still have a responsibility to them and need to observe them. Obviously you won't have such a large and detailed record on that child, but they need to be included in the process as well.

You plan for the benefit of the children and the setting

You might have annotations on your plans in this instance as it can be difficult to plan in advance, so you need to be flexible and responsive.

I've tried to make contact with another setting a child attends to discuss their progress but I'm getting nowhere!

As long as you've tried and documented that you have tried, and keep trying that is fine. Remember this doesn't have to be anything formal, maybe just a brief chat every half term over the phone.

I am behind with my observations and I can't catch up.

It is always a problem, when you get behind, to catch up and it means

that the children are missing out because you haven't been able to respond to the observations.

However, sometimes things happen and when you do get behind the best thing to do is to find any evidence you can from the missing time such as photos and file these for the child, then start the observations again afresh. You cannot do observations retrospectively, you will just have to miss this time and try not to get behind again. This may mean you are doing too many observations. Remember it is about quality not quantity and capturing key moments.

I have so many sticky labels that I don't know what to do with them.

This would indicate that the labels

are not being used in a way that is appropriate for purpose.

When taking observations on sticky labels (or any short observation) make sure that you are going to use it for some purpose. Sometimes it is possible to hold information in our heads and not need to write every single thing down.

I find that there are so many pieces of paper and so much information that I don't know what to use.

This seems to indicate that your systems are way too complicated and unmanageable. Try to simplify them so that you and other people can understand them and use them effectively.

I don't feel my staff team are working with an effective system of observations and planning.

If a leader or manager gets sense of this, the first question to ask is why? Could it be that practitioners don't understand the system, or feel they lack knowledge and skills? Whole staff training maybe required or better support maybe necessary.

It could be that the system you are attempting to implement might be over-complicated. Don't just be dismissive: look at what the root causes are of this problem.

I'm under constant pressure from parents/ carers for their child to be able to write their name.

This is a common problem, the first thing to remember is that you are there for the children and not the parents or guardians.

You need to focus on your knowledge and understanding of good early years practice and explain to parents how

Working together makes the process of observing and planning much easier

children need to develop fine motor and manipulative skills first before being able to control a pencil to write their name.

It is clear in the 'Development Matters' document, looking at the specific area of literacy, that the key emphasis is on understanding language and fine motor skills first and writing comes second.

How do I know if my observation is informative for assessment?

Reflect on your observation and see if you can answer the questions 'what I have I learnt about the child?'. 'What do I know now I didn't know before?'.

Observation and planning and your Ofsted inspection

During an Ofsted inspection, the inspector will be looking at noting various aspects of paperwork and the children's progress, these notes are to help you be aware of what they may look for:

How an inspector may observe practitioners interacting with and supporting the children.

1. The inspector should observe whether adult interactions are merely concerned with supervising children or whether adults motivate children and engage them in activities. In particular, the inspector should evaluate whether adults' questions challenge children to think and find out more by encouraging them to speculate and test ideas through trial and error. They should also assess whether adults model language well, develop children's ability to express their ideas and extend their use of new words. The inspector should identify what children can do by themselves and what they can do when supported by a practitioner.

2. Equally important are times when practitioners leave children alone to explore, make their own discoveries, solve problems and learn skills through self-initiated play. The inspector should evaluate the skill of practitioners by observing how and when adults intervene in children's play.

3. The inspector should not routinely expect to see detailed written plans for the activities they observe, although they must look at plans when they are offered by practitioners. The inspector should focus on the overall quality of the approach and whether the planning, interventions and evaluation of activities ensure there is a consistent approach to teaching and learning. This will enable them to identify the most important areas for improvement in relation to children's learning and progress.

During an inspection two, possibly more, children will be tracked by an inspector.

Their case tracking will include:

- Observation notes, assessment and planning for each child including the progress check for any children aged two.

- Discussions with each child's key person and information about progress over time.

- Any records kept by the provision that show how they have tracked the progress children make, including any concerns about the children's development in the prime and/or specific areas of learning.

- An evaluation of the accuracy and rigour of the provision's assessments and the extent to which children's next steps in learning are well planned.

They will observe the tracked children so they can evaluate:

- The range of activities children take part in, whether solitary, self-initiated or adult initiated.

- The quality and timeliness of adults' interventions.

- The level of challenge of the activities for the children's age/stage of development.

The inspector judging children's progress

1. Children's progress should not be viewed as a 'race to the goals'. The extent of children's progress relates mainly to the quality of teaching and the impact this has on children's progress. Where the practitioner has a good knowledge about each child's learning and development, this is a characteristic of effective teaching.

2. Any evaluation of children's progress towards the early learning goals must be judged in relation to

their starting points, their individual needs, how long they have been at the provision and how often they attend. The inspector should examine the information that the provision gathers about what children know, can do and enjoy when they start to attend. Evidence of starting points can also be gained by talking with staff and parents about the level of children's social, communication and physical skills on entry, and, importantly, by observing children new to the provision.

3. The inspector must use the evidence to evaluate how well the provider and practitioners know about, and understand, the progress children are making towards the early learning goals. The inspector must judge whether adults have appropriately high expectations for children. In particular, the inspector must judge whether gaps for children who are disadvantaged are narrowing and whether children are performing at expected levels of development. The inspector must consider:

■ How well the provider and practitioners know and understand the Early Years Foundation Stage learning and development requirements.

■ How and when parents are asked for information about their child's development.

■ How often practitioners share a summary of their observations of children with the children's parents, and their plans for reviewing children's progress at age two.

■ Whether practitioners can reliably identify children whose learning and development is not at the expected developmental band, whether those children are working at a level above or below the expected level and what actions they have taken to ensure those children make sufficient progress.

■ Any changes made to activities/resources/routines/the environment as a result of observations and subsequent evaluations of the impact of those changes.

■ The involvement of the SENCO where there are concerns about a child's development and learning.

Taken from 'Conducting Early Years Inspections' Ofsted November 2014 (120087)

Birth to 2-year-old summative assessment

Included on the CD-Rom

Name of child: ....

Date: .... Age: ....

Completed by: ....

How long attended setting: ....

Pattern of attendance: ....

Personal, Social and Emotional Development	Communication and Language	Physical Development
Development phase	Development phase	Development phase
Specific Areas	Characteristics of Effective Learning	Key Interests

Next Steps:

....

....

....

Parent/Carer Comment:

....

....

....

The progress check at two

Name of child: _____

Date of birth: _____ Age: _____

Date: _____

How long attended setting: _____

Pattern of attendance: _____

PERSONAL, SOCIAL AND EMOTIONAL DEVELOPMENT	COMMUNICATION AND LANGUAGE	PHYSICAL DEVELOPMENT
Making relationships:	Listening and attention:	Moving and handling:
Development phase	Development phase	Development phase
Self confidence and self awareness:	Understanding:	Health and self care:
Development phase	Development phase	Development phase
Managing feelings and behaviour:	Speaking:	
Development phase	Development phase	
Parent comment:	Parent comment:	Parent/Carer comment:

Child's interests:

_____

_____

_____

Together we have decided the next steps to support learning and development (home and setting):

_____

_____

_____

Key person signature: _____ Date: _____

Parent/Carer signature: _____ Date: _____

Further resources

Publications

Early Years Foundation Stage Statutory Framework (DfE 2014)

Right From The Start Early Years Good Practice Films: Assessment (Ofsted 2014)

Early Years Outcomes (DfE 2013)

Development Matters (DfE 2012)

Good Practice Resource – 'Child-initiated learning in the Early Years' (Ofsted 2012)

Good Practice Resource – 'An innovative approach to observing and assessing children's learning and development' (Ofsted 2012)

Finding and Exploring Young Children's Fascinations – Strengthening the Quality of Gifted and Talented Provision in the Early Years (DCSF 2010)

Children Thinking Mathematically: PSRN Essential Knowledge for Early Years Practitioners (DCSF 2010)

Inclusion Development Programme: 'Supporting Children with Behavioural, Emotional and Social Difficulties: Guidance for Practitioners in the Early Years Foundation Stage' (DCSF 2010)

Challenging Practice to Further Improve Learning, Playing and Interacting in the Early Years Foundation Stage (DCSF 2010)

Childminding: A Passion to be Outstanding (Ofsted 2009)

Childcare Groups: A Passion to be Outstanding (Ofsted 2009)

Progress Matters: Reviewing and Enhancing Young Children's Development (DCSF 2009)

Learning, Playing and Interacting: Good Practice in the Early Years Foundation Stage (DCSF 2009)

Inclusion Development Programme: 'Supporting Children on the Autism Spectrum: Guidance for Practitioners in the Early Years Foundation Stage' (2009)

Mark Making Matters: Young Children Making Meaning in all Areas of Learning and Development (DCSF 2008)

Inclusion Development Programme: 'Supporting Children with speech, language and communication needs: Guidance for practitioners in the Early Years Foundation Stage' (DCSF 2008)

Social and Emotional Aspects of Development: Guidance for practitioners working in the Early Years Foundation Stage (DCSF 2008)

Supporting children learning English as an additional language (DCSF 2007)

Confident, capable and creative: supporting boys' achievements (DCSF 2007)

KEEP (Key Elements of Effective Practice) (DFES 2005)

Starting With Quality: The Rumbold Report (DES 1989)

Bruce, T. (1997) *Early Childhood Education*, Hodder and Stoughton, London

Websites

www.ofsted.gov.uk

www.foundationyears.org.uk

www.education.gov.uk